CERC Monograph
International Educat

G000244458

Education, Growth, Aid and Development

Towards Education for All

Edited by
Linda Chisholm, Graeme Bloch & Brahm Fleisch

Comparative Education Research Centre
The University of Hong Kong

Southern African Review of Education
Southern African Comparative and History of Education Society

First published 2008
Comparative Education Research Centre
Faculty of Education
The University of Hong Kong
Pokfulam Road, Hong Kong, China

In collaboration with the
Southern African Comparative and History of Education Society (SACHES)

© Comparative Education Research Centre

ISBN 978 962 8093 99 1

This monograph contains five articles that were originally published in the *Southern African Review of Education*, Volume 13, Number 2, of 2007. Permission to reprint these articles has been granted by the Southern African Comparative and History of Education Society, publishers of the *Southern African Review of Education*. This permission is gratefully acknowledged.

Cover design: Vincent Lee

Cover photograph: Bjorn Nordtveit

Layout: Emily Mang

Contents

List of Abbreviations and Acronyms

CREATE	Consortium for Research on Educational Access, Transitions and Equity
DAC	Development Assistance Committee
DBSA	Development Bank of Southern Africa
DESD	Decade of Education for Sustainable Development
DFID	Department for International Development (UK)
EDI	Education for All Development Index
EFA	Education for All
ESD	education for sustainable development
FTI	Fast Track Initiative
GAD	gender and development
GDP	Gross Domestic Product
GERs	gross enrolment rates
GMR	Global Monitoring Report
HSRC	Human Sciences Research Council
IDTs	International Development Targets
ILO	International Labour Organization
IMF	International Monetary Fund
OECD	Organisation for Economic Co-operation and Development
MDGs	Millennium Development Goals
NERS	net enrolment rates
NGOs	Non-Governmental Organisations
PBET	post-basic education and training
SDs	standard deviations
SSA	sub-Saharan Africa
TIMSS	Third [also Trends in] International Mathematics and Science Study
TVSD	technical and vocational skills development
UN	United Nations
UNCTAD	United Nations Conference on Trade and Development
UNDP	United Nations Development Programme
UNESCO	United Nations Educational, Cultural and Scientific Organization
UPE	universal primary education
WID	women in development

List of Tables

List of Figures

Series Editor's Foreword

The Universal Declaration of Human Rights, adopted by the United Nations in 1948, states unequivocally that everyone has the right to education. Yet there are still some 72 million children around the world who are out of school, and 774 million adults who are not able to read or write. The situation in 2000 – when 96 million children were out of school – was even worse, and, to mark the turn of the millennium, 164 countries committed themselves, at the World Education Forum in Dakar in Senegal, to achieve by 2015 six goals, known by their aim to achieve "Education for All" (EFA), that would vastly improve learning opportunities for children, youth and adults. These goals were to (1) expand early childhood care and education; (2) provide free and compulsory primary education for all; (3) promote learning and life skills for young people and adults; (4) increase adult literacy by 50 per cent; (5) achieve gender parity by 2005, and gender equality by 2015; and (6) improve the quality of education.

The EFA Global Monitoring Report (GMR) produces a regular assessment of the progress that countries are making towards the realization of these goals. It is no coincidence that one of this volume's contributing authors, Christopher Colclough, was the founding Director of the Global Monitoring Report on Education for All. The 2008 report makes sobering reading, given that it marks the halfway point to 2015. The deadline to achieve gender parity by 2005 has been missed (in south and west Asia, for example, two thirds of those children who are not in school are girls), and the latest GMR indicates that although there has been some progress in providing care and education for very young children, what has been achieved is, at this halfway point, far from satisfactory. The report acknowledges that substantial progress has been made in improving access to primary school, but indicates that a wide gap remains between enrolment and completion rates, especially for children from the poorest households and marginalized groups in society. The GMR warns further that concerns about the quality of education are emerging everywhere. This mid-term review shows, say the report's authors, "that the comprehensive vision of the Dakar agenda is in danger of being lost". Countries are paying only minimal attention to adult literacy needs and to early childhood care and education. In many countries, fees and indirect costs of education remain a major obstacle to schooling for the poorest children. These indirect costs include the opportunity cost of sending a child to school who is then unable, for example, to help tend the family's animals or their subsistence farming plot. To achieve Education for All, the report suggests that "efforts need to be accelerated and more focused, with donors also making a greater effort to align themselves with national policies". Public spending on basic education clearly needs to increase.

The EFA goals were of course set deliberately high, not just because that was the spirit at the turn of the millennium, but in order to focus the world's attention on the appalling violations of the right to education that were, and still are, evident across the world. Many must have quietly realized all along that these were very ambitious goals, but that doesn't mean that governments shouldn't be working as hard as possible to reach them. Francoise Caillods of UNESCO's International Institute for Educational Planning (IIEP) has recently sketched some of the factors that are slowing down progress towards EFA: crises and conflict, HIV and AIDS, extreme poverty, and bad governance. Lack of finance is often mentioned as a constraint, but it is not the only one, nor, she maintains, the most important. Lack of political will, little capacity to manage funds and implement policies, and corruption are other serious impediments.

As editor of this book series focused on educational development, I'm not so sure that the GMR should in every case be encouraging donors to make greater efforts to align themselves with the national policies of the countries with which they work. To do so without questioning the budgetary priorities of some governments would amount to tacit endorsement of some questionable political and policy decisions. The uncomfortable truth is that many governments around the world are still not placing EFA high enough on their policy agendas. By diverting spending to huge military expansion, South Africa's government, for example, opens itself to accusations of tokenism in what it is really doing to redress the imbalances of Apartheid education. A recent report indicates that poverty has doubled in that country in the last 10 years – this in the face of obscene military spending.

By diverting massive resources to a space programme aimed at 'national pride and prestige', China opens itself to the same accusations. To be true, China has made impressive strides in improving adult literacy, but it is hard to see how vast spending on getting a Chinese astronaut onto the moon can be justified. China would earn far more international prestige if it were to follow the example of a country like Cuba and place its resources squarely in education in order really to provide Education for All. Cuba is exemplary in this regard: through its policy – and practice – of universal basic education, it has achieved about the highest rates of literacy in the world. The country has one teacher for every 37 inhabitants. More than this, schools play a central role in the provision of social and welfare services. Children are provided with a nutritious cooked lunch at school. Schools function as day care centres for children from families where both parents work, and day care specialists are at school from very early in the morning and again until late into the evening. Apart from the human rights that China would so honour, it would find its reservoir of human capital, to use a rather unfortunate metaphor, substantially increased, and its global economic competitiveness correspondingly enhanced.

The IIEP's Caillods suggests that it is necessary to increase the capacity of central governments to, *inter alia*, design policies and reforms, and to allocate resources. Strengthening the state, making it efficient and responsive, she suggests, is a major challenge for the years ahead. Even more important than this, I would suggest, are the political and budgetary priorities set by governments. Governments the world over are notorious for responding to the demands of elites, of the wealthy and powerful, in their society, and for neglecting the basic needs of the great majority of their citizens. It is these citizens who need to demand of their governments that the EFA goals be placed centre-stage, and to hold their leaders publicly accountable when their spending priorities are wasted on the vainglorious pursuit of the likes of military prestige or putting somebody on the moon. For every child's life wasted, such policies are a disgrace.

In this spirit, I welcome this volume into the *CERC Monograph Series in Comparative and International Education and Development*. The challenges are substantial, the indications that we are not doing enough ominous. This monograph offers a timely and valuable contribution that might help to reinvigorate and renew commitments to the achievement of Education for All.

Mark MASON

Editor
CERC Monograph Series in Comparative and International Education and Development

Director
Comparative Education Research Centre
The University of Hong Kong

Preface

Linda CHISHOLM

This monograph brings together a number of chapters by leading authors in the field of education and development. They draw on decades of research and personal experience to assess what we have learnt from research over three decades on school effects, the utility and sustainability of target-setting in education, and the role of global and local forces in shaping change in African education. Four of these five chapters were first presented at a conference on Investment Choices for Education in Africa, held at the University of the Witwatersrand, Johannesburg, in September 2006.[1] And another, fortuitously on a similar set of issues, was presented at the UK Forum for International Education and Training Conference in Oxford in September 2007. The chapters are significant for two reasons: first, because they reflect the cumulative wisdom of five remarkable scholars, and second, because they each either explicitly or implicitly raise questions about the targets and benchmarks associated with the Education For All (EFA) initiatives and the Millennium Development Goals (MDGs).

Each author has made a substantial contribution over time to learning about education in Africa. It would be hard to single out any one of these writers for their contribution; the oeuvre of each spans a sustained interest in the relationships not only among education, growth and development, but in the role of education in societies characterised by wealth and poverty. Each of the authors has made landmark contributions that have shaped writing about and in Africa for decades. They all, in one way or another, have a long acquaintance with educational issues in Eastern and Southern Africa particularly. Kenneth King's influential and pioneering Pan-Africanism and Education: A Study of Race Philanthropy in the Southern States of America and East Africa (1971) shaped subsequent work in the field in fundamental ways. Carnoy's monumental work, Education as Cultural Imperialism (1974), was also inspired by work in Kenya. His interests subsequently moved to Latin America and the United States of America. But here he turns his eye to lessons learned from work over several decades in developing countries. Dani Nabudere has also for many years cast a refreshing eye on questions related to development and democracy, and the state and economic development. Christopher Colclough and Keith Lewin have both had a long and close collaboration on African education, with a special interest in Southern and Eastern African education. Christopher Colclough's role as founding Director of UNESCO's EFA Global Monitoring Report has been highly significant for the region. Keith Lewin's rich contribution to understanding the challenges of development in African education, and especially the implications of EFA for secondary schooling provision, are informed by wider experience, in his case of China and Asia.

Carnoy's wide-ranging chapter opens this monograph. Drawing on his work in Latin America, it provides a state of the art review of the evidence of different strategies to improve school quality and educational performance and the trade-offs to be made between investing in educational quantity or quality. As such it raises complex questions about the expectations of target-setters. Distinguishing between educational achievement and attainment, his chapter exposes to critical scrutiny a number of educational shibboleths: improving quality at basic education level when there are no places at secondary level; the use of repetition and drop out data as measures of quality in the context of large classes in developing countries; the inadequacy of tests as a measure of what students learn; student achievement as a principal measure of school output; the inconclusive evidence of randomised field trials or intervention research in raising test scores; the conundrum of no improvement in maths and science test scores in OECD countries between 1970 and 1994; and whether it is lack of competition between schools that results in lack of quality, or simply "the lack of quality teachers and management". "Whether private or public", he argues, "schools cannot implement challenging curricula if teachers have low levels of subject knowledge and have little understanding of how to teach those curricula".

He concludes that there is no quick fix for educational quality in developing countries, and that the path countries have historically taken is to improve student performance through improving student attainment or increasing the number of years they stay in school. Ultimately, improving performance is expensive: it requires a demanding curriculum and well-trained teachers who believe in their students and who are supervised in a way that enables them to achieve high levels of competence and to show up daily to teach. Improving attainment through increasing the number of years in school is more feasible and less expensive than, for example, improving the quality at specific levels of education through reducing class sizes.

Central to the strategies that Carnoy discusses are the interventions of the development aid community. Christopher Colclough focuses on the failures of international aid processes since 2000 to produce significant change. Writing from the experience of being Editor of the authoritative EFA Global Monitoring Report from 2002 to 2005, and therefore central to many of the debates and discussions of the international community in these target-setting and investment planning processes, he argues that the target-setting process is unrealistic in its ignoring of both history and context. The simple appearance of the goals belies the complexity of the tasks to be accomplished. It is often assumed in the international community that the answer lies in either "plugging the financial gaps" or adopting "simple policy measures". Laudable as the goals and commitments are, another difficulty is holding national governments and the international community to their promises. Donors have failed to take advantage of the Fast Track Initiative, promised additional resources have not been delivered, and the financial muscle of UNESCO has been too weak to achieve policy leverage.

Whereas Colclough's critique draws on his experience of multi- and bi-lateral development agency processes of target-setting, the importance of Keith Lewin's chapter lies in his close analysis of actual targets and benchmarks in specific contexts. His analysis reveals the arbitrary nature of the selection of targets, the different types and methods of measuring targets, the incentives for choosing definitions of targets that enable the manipulation of data to show they have been achieved, the lack of a sense of national ownership, the scope for confusion, and the potentially negative and unrealistic implications and consequences of and trade-offs between having different types of targets. He concludes that while targets may have a value, they can also distort the development process. The implications of his article are that targets need to be feasible, balanced and nationally owned.

Kenneth King extends the critical analysis of targets and bench-marks by taking the argument from the educational to the labour market terrain and from improving aid to reducing dependence. He argues that, while there has been some very detailed work on analyzing progress towards the MDGs, much less attention has been given to the sustain-ability of these externally-assisted achievements. He asks whether indi-vidual countries will be able to sustain the reforms initiated with deve-lopment aid when it ceases, and whether they have economic and po-litical environments that will help them to reach the MDGs. He asks what is available in the labour market for millions of young people who have been persuaded to enter school on the basis of the benefits it will bring. In so doing, he returns us to the critical question of the labour market context of schooling, the nature of work that pertains in the ur-ban and rural informal economies, and the character of economic growth. The article restores a balance to a discussion that is often too inward-looking.

In this context of global multi- and bi-lateral implementation fail-ure, discussion of the developmental state in Africa becomes particu-larly significant. If the challenges are substantial and the international commitments hard to implement, then the role of the national state to pursue economic and development objectives becomes all the more important. The concept of the developmental state emerged in the con-text of the International Financial Institutions' strident promotion of markets at the expense of states during the 1980s and 1990s. Drawing on the experience of the Asian miracle, the developmental state was held up as being able to compensate for market failures in the new, more revisionist approach of the "post Washington Consensus".

Dani Nabudere's chapter examines the concept and the possibili-ties of the realisation of the developmental state in relation to Africa. He shows how African states "became permanently tied to external sources of finance whatever economic activity they planned for their countries" at the very moment that Asian developmental states moved towards greater independence through export-oriented industrialisation. He as-cribes this to three successive colonial occupations, the third occurring through structural adjustment, the idealisation of the market and private initiative over the post-colonial state, and the promotion of good gov-ernance and accountability as the new ideology of the "market-state".

He argues for "the glocal state" through the building and harnessing of social capital in the form of informal sector and community-based savings and pension funds. Investing in opportunities for "learning to learn", he argues, is critical to the achievement of a learning economy and a "glocal" developmental state.

This monograph, in conclusion, presents a rich set of reflections on development thought and practice at the start of the twentieth century, representing the cumulative wisdom and judgment of scholars who have made an indelible mark on educational thought. They present a formidable set of conceptual, practical and political challenges for consideration by the development world in its target-setting processes, especially in the field of education.

¹ A selection of papers from this conference was published in the *Southern African Review of Education* 13 (2) 2007. The organizing partners for the conference were the Human Sciences Research Council (HSRC), the Wits School of Education and the Development Bank of Southern Africa (DBSA). Funding was provided by the European Union CWCI Fund.

Lessons from the past two decades: Investment choices for education and growth

Martin CARNOY

One of the largest expenditures a modern nation makes is on the education of its people. How much it spends and how it spends its resources to provide education can have an influence on economic and social outcomes – economic growth, income distribution, social mobility and the society's sense of wellbeing. In this chapter, I review some of the important decisions that governments make regarding educational spending and educational delivery. I focus on the possible trade-off between investing in educational quality and quantity and in various strategies that are associated with increasing the amount of education that young people take and in the quality of the education they receive. I also discuss the implications of educational financing choices and choices about the organisation of educational delivery.

The economic context

Education represents both a right and need, and occupies a central role in the determination of individual standards of living. People's health and happiness, their economic security, opportunities and social status – each is affected by education. Education is also a major determinant of the welfare of nations, as the sum of micro-level individual educational experiences has important implications for macro conditions in the society as a whole. Because of its importance in these processes, education is often at the centre of policy discussions about human development.

Part of the crucial role education plays in improving quality of life is manifested in the economic arena. This is especially the case today, where an increasingly globalised economy places a higher premium on economic competitiveness than before, and, increasingly, because of new information technologies, economic growth and social development depend on human knowledge rather than the availability of natural resources. These new and rapidly changing conditions in an increasingly interdependent world economy require more flexible, easily trainable labour better able to access and interpret the mass of information available. This, in turn, requires higher quality, more adaptable education able to provide young people and adults with the knowledge and life skills to function effectively in the new environment. Nations with more educated populations are also more likely to develop better organised, more cohesive civil societies – the social capital underpinning economic and social development in the new information, global society.

Nations are therefore under much greater pressure than in the past to expand education and increase its quality to develop the highly skilled labour forces and social capital needed to compete in the global economy. Nations are also under pressure from families striving to give their children an advantage in an increasingly competitive environment around getting good jobs. As such competition intensifies, there is an increasing tendency toward inequality and inequity of access to good education. International agencies are also pressuring countries to meet internationally set goals for universal primary education and adult literacy. And because most countries do not have the public resources to meet all these demands, they are under pressure to reduce costs or, at the least, to raise the cost-effectiveness of their public education investments. This often means turning to a mixture of financing (private/ public), which has implications for both equity and effectiveness. In these conditions, what are the best strategies for meeting new demands in education? How should countries think about delivering higher quality education and more years of education to their populations, especially their young populations?

Every country faces a different set of initial economic and political conditions as it confronts the global economy in the information age. Some economies are mainly agricultural, and others industrialised, already transitioning to a service economy. Some countries have highly developed civil societies. Others do not. So each situation demands its own particular strategy for educational expansion and improvement.

Globalisation increases returns to higher levels of education, hence pressure for more education and for more rapid expansion of higher secondary and university education. Of course, in many countries with large rural populations, expanding and reducing dropouts in primary education will remain a major concern. But even there, the pressures for expanding secondary education will increase. Two of the main issues for planners will be how to expand these more expensive types of schooling effectively and how to ensure that access to higher levels is not limited to the already most advantaged groups in society. Thus, for each level of economic development, investing in the level of education generally attended by youth from middle-income families in that country is associated with the greatest contribution to economic growth. This means that in the earlier stages of economic development, primary education is characterised by high economic rates of return, and, as an economy begins to become industrialised and the educational system expands, rates of return to secondary education rise and rates to primary fall. In the past 25 years, the rates of return to university education have been rising relative to other levels throughout the world, and in many countries are higher than rates to lower levels of schooling.[1]

Yet a significant proportion of the youth population in middle-income and high-income countries attends these lower levels of schooling. At the same time that economic competitiveness considerations are pressuring many middle and high-income developing countries to focus on expanding higher levels of education, equity considerations are pushing them to focus on expanding and improving basic education. From an equity perspective, the social good (as measured, for example, by improved children's health and nutrition, lower fertility rates, a better functioning civil society) increases more from public spending on basic education than on higher levels (Carnoy, 1993). In terms of improving the social conditions of the greatest number of children, it may be more 'efficient' to invest scarce public resources at the primary level, shifting them away from subsidising secondary and particularly university education. This is the position of the Education for All programme, and many countries that are already competing in world markets in more technologically sophisticated goods and services (India and Brazil, for example), and so are very concerned with the quantity and quality of university graduates, also need to be concerned with bringing reasonable quality primary education to the majority of the school age population that is not completing that level.

From an economic growth perspective, then, countries like Brazil, Mexico and South Africa should probably be investing heavily in university education and high-quality secondary education that prepares increasing numbers of students for university-level work. Yet, if the private rate of return is high to attending university, and the externalities are relatively low (medical education in South Africa might be such a case, since many medical graduates emigrate), the payment for such education should be at least partially (and perhaps largely) private. Public funding could then be allocated to increasing the quality of education at lower levels of schooling (externalities of greater equity) and to providing higher levels of education in fields of study that have lower private rates of return but high social rates of return – teachers might fall into this category. Thus, investment choices are often influenced by educational financing arrangements.

Because work will increasingly be organised around multi-tasking and workers will hold a number of different jobs during their work careers (Carnoy 2000), planners should also reconsider long-held views about the balance between vocational and general education. As education expands to ever-higher levels, the nature of different levels, particularly secondary, changes as well, becoming increasingly preparatory for post-secondary, and vocational education moves out of the secondary to post-secondary level. Both these shifts should alter the organisation and objectives of secondary schooling.

Quantity and quality of education
The most prevalent discussion of educational investment strategies is about how much spending on various *levels* of education contributes to economic growth and equity. However, a more recent trend is to discuss the contribution to growth of investing in higher student achievement at a given level of education (Hanushek and Kimko 2000; EFA 2005; Hanushek and Wößmann 2006).

The issue of investing in achievement versus attainment is important for two reasons that we explore in the rest of this chapter. The more traditional approach of setting educational quantitative goals for the world's children is almost certainly a more meaningful educational objective in terms of improving people's lives than raising test scores (quality) in a given grade. Raising quality in the poorest performing schools is related to increasing the educational attainment of low-income children *as long as there are sufficient places at the next highest level of schooling to accommodate them.* Further, the economy behaves as if it cares much more about the level of schooling attained than the test scores achieved *per se.* For example, estimates in the United States using longitudinal data show that the payoff in increased wages to higher achievement scores for high school graduates who do not go on to college is negligible, and the payoff in increased wages for college graduates is only eight per cent more income for a full standard deviation higher achievement score (Carnoy and DeAngelis 2000). As we would expect, the main payoff to higher achievement derives from the greater likelihood that those who score higher go further in school, hence earn higher income.

Second, raising test scores in a given grade, while certainly contributing to higher-quality education and student learning, may be a more costly way to increase the amount students learn than increasing the number of years they stay in school. As the 2005 EFA report argued, it appears that there is a positive economic return to increased achievement (about eight to nine per cent higher wages for a one standard deviation increase in test scores), but there are few proven educational strategies that can increase test scores by even 0,3 of a standard deviation. If this reasoning is correct, the optimum strategy would be to find the least expensive ways to raise student test scores in the context of increasing student attainment. Using recent comparative research, we will argue that there may be some effective ways to do that, and also many dead ends.

One of the most interesting results of the international tests over time is that no OECD country has made significant increases in their maths and science scores in the period 1970-1994. Lant Pritchett (2003) suggests that despite large increases in educational spending per pupil, scores have not risen. Mathematics test scores have risen in recent years in the United States in both the 4th and 8th grades (Carnoy and Loeb 2003) and minorities made large gains in maths and reading in all grades in the late 1970s and 1980s relative to whites (Carnoy 1994), so it is possible to make gains, but apparently not easily. Similarly, test scores on the national SIMCE test in Chile in both the 4th and 8th grades have not risen significantly since 1996, when the bi-annual tests were made comparable. Chile also made very large increases in spending per pupil during this period for very much the same reason – teacher salaries went up considerably.

Table 1.1 Changes in maths and science scores on international tests and changes in real spending per pupil, by country, 1970-1994 (%)

Country	Estimated Change in Maths and Science Score, 1970-1994 (%)	Estimated Change in Real Spending per Pupil, 1970-1994 (%)
Sweden	4,3	28,5
United States	0,0	33,1
The Netherlands	1,7	36,3
Belgium	-4,7	64,7
United Kingdom	-8,2	76,7
Japan	-1,9	103,3
Germany	-4,8	108,1
Italy	1,3	125,7
France	-6,6	211,6
New Zealand	-9,7	222,5
Australia	-2,3	269,8

Source: Pritchett 2003

Why have countries had such a difficult time increasing average test scores? Pritchett comes up with several possible reasons, including the impact of television on children and their use of time and changes in pedagogy toward 'softer,' less test-oriented teaching methods. However, our observations in a number of countries, both developed and developing, suggest three other major explanations: a student composition effect, a teacher capacity effect, and a managerial capacity effect.

The socio-economic composition of students is changing in every school system. As each level of schooling expands, more children from a lower socio-economic background are drawn into the level, and less educated parents have more children, on average, than more educated parents. In every country we have observed, the process has been the same. Enrolment increases rapidly in primary school, then secondary, then university, and at each level, as enrolment goes up, the average parental education of students in that level begins to decline. In addition, changing population composition among the young changes student composition in school. In the past 25 years in the developed countries, particularly in the more 'open' ones, such as the US, Australia, New Zealand, Canada and Great Britain, the enormous influx of immigrants from developing countries combined with declining birth rates among more educated natives has contributed to this effect. Now this immigration has spread to most of Western Europe and even Japan. In the developing countries, declining birth rates among the more educated has been a major factor in transforming the student population in school.

Other tendencies also exist. Continued emigration from rural to urban areas changes the average environment for developing nation schools. In general, this change seems to have a beneficial effect on test scores. For example, once parents' education and other resources are accounted for, children in Latin American rural schools tend to score lower than children in urban areas (Carnoy and Marshall 2003). Better communications, more access to academic resources, and other factors in an urban environment seem to have a positive effect on student achievement.

Given these compositional changes, it is somewhat remarkable that educational systems have been able to bring increasing numbers of pupils into ever higher levels of schooling *without* much decline in test scores. This accomplishment suggests that educational systems are able to absorb 'higher-cost' children into the system by spending more per pupil, but that spending more per pupil does not necessarily increase the performance of the average performing pupil. Thus, the difficulty of increasing the test scores of average students in a country should not be confused with increasing student performance of students at the bottom of the performance ladder. Systems can improve the performance of low-performing groups mainly by making the conditions of their schools more like the schools attended by higher-performing children. We discuss this in more detail below, but there is good evidence from Chile and Argentina (Carnoy et al 2003) and from the *Escuela Nueva* programme in Colombia (McEwan 1999) that more and better resources for low-income schools have a positive impact on student achievement.

The problem for the 'average' student in a particular level of schooling is different, since that student already gets average resources. Apparently, improving this student's performance requires changing something about the way the system delivers education, and this is where serious difficulties arise. The two main difficulties we have observed are teacher and manager capacity. Without improving teacher skills, including subject matter knowledge and pedagogical skills, it has proved difficult to improve teaching, and without better teaching it is difficult to improve student academic achievement. This is easier said than done, since increasing teacher content knowledge requires a large investment in teachers' maths and language skills or recruiting a different group of people to be teachers.

The second major obstacle to improved student performance is managerial capacity. Teachers in most developing countries are largely autonomous, learn on the job without supervision, and are often absent from the classroom, especially in rural areas. Unlike other industries, education is not management-intensive. School directors and even pedagogical coordinators rarely gather data on the performance of teachers, either directly, by observing their teaching in the classroom, or by analyzing student performance gains in each class.

The reasons for this are complex, but the most persuasive ones are that school principals are usually not expected to be instructional leaders and do not have the skills to take that role even if they were supposed to.

Improving the quality of education
Any investment strategy that purports to improve educational quality has to define the operational meaning of quality. Before assessing 'what works' to improve education, policy-makers need to decide what school outputs they want to see increased. Most analysts discuss quality in terms of student achievement, for good reason. All schools assess students based on examinations, projects, behaviour in class and effort. Student achievement therefore seems to be the primary product schools intend to produce. Whether or not student performance on tests is actually a good measure of educational system quality, it has come to *symbolize* quality.

However, student achievement per se is not the only measure of school quality. Since many pupils in low-income countries are made to repeat grades and often drop out of school (this also happens in secondary school in developed countries), analysts have used these repetition and dropout data as an indicator of educational quality, arguing implicitly that teacher evaluations represent some 'external standard' of student performance and repetitions and dropouts represent a measure of the system's ability to reach that standard.

In some ways, repetition and dropouts are good indicators of educational quality. If a teacher is unable to teach pupils to read or to add and subtract simple numbers in the first grade, those pupils in much of the world fail the grade and are made to repeat it. If they do not learn to read the second time around, they are likely to drop out. The higher the percentage of repeaters and dropouts, the worse the system is at reaching its academic objectives. However, from another perspective, repetition and dropouts are misleading indicators of the quality or efficiency of the system. I visited many schools in former French West and Central Africa with more than 100 pupils in each of several first grade classrooms. There were simply not enough or big enough classrooms in the school to accommodate those pupils were a high percentage of them to continue on to second, third or fourth grade. Many rural multi-grade schools in Latin America have one or two teachers with students from first to fourth or sixth grade. The available space in those schools does not permit all students to complete all the grades. So, in those African or rural Latin American schools there is an expectation, even a need, to fail pupils. Even in cases where there is room for everyone, there may not be an upper primary (4th to 6th grades) or lower secondary school (7th to 9th grades) available in walking distance. Students begin dropping out in primary school because pupils and their parents perceive correctly that there is no further education available. It is no accident that repetition and dropout rates fall in primary school when sufficient secondary school places start becoming available for the entire age cohort.

Thus, repetition and dropout rates can be in some sense accurate but also inaccurate measures of educational quality. If primary schools are unable to retain pupils, they are clearly failing to teach them the required curriculum. Yet, at the same time, there is little incentive for teachers to exert themselves or try to be effective if there are only enough places for a few successful pupils to go on. And if there is no place for promoted pupils, the system may, in a perverse fashion, be 'efficiently' pushing out those pupils who cannot 'get it' on their own. Is this a conspiracy? Not really. If not enough resources exist to produce high-quality education for everyone, the system becomes highly selective rather than one that tries to help everyone learn. Teachers become presenters of material and not much more. Michel Welmond's research in Benin, Cameroon and Chad, for example, suggests that teachers in French-speaking West Africa see themselves primarily as civil servants responsible for *presenting* the curriculum to pupils and acting as a *phare* (light) for the community, not for pupils' academic success (Welmond 2002). In their view, this is the family's role.

Thus, student achievement in a given grade has come to symbolise quality, but, as we argued earlier, the main drawback to using test scores in a *given* grade as a measure of educational quality is that they fail to account for how many years children go to school in that particular educational system. Success rates in school can also measure educational quality. For example, eighth graders in the US score lower on the TIMSS mathematics test than their counterparts in the Czech Republic. But a much higher percentage of the age cohort in the US completes university than in the Czech Republic, and, on average, four-year universities in the US are as good as those in the Czech Republic. Which educational system is higher quality? Which helps its nation become more competitive economically? This is not a simple question, but we can say that just because US eighth graders do not do as well as Czech eighth graders on maths tests this does not translate into lower productivity for the average US worker. Similarly, Brazilian 15-year-olds did much better on the PISA test than Peruvian 15-year-olds, but a Peruvian 15-year-old is much more likely to finish high school and continue on to university than a Brazilian 15-year-old. In which system are students doing better?

A second well-known drawback is that the quality of an educational system or a school should not be measured in terms of the absolute scores of its students, but rather in terms of what the school or the system *adds* to the students' learning. By the time they are six or seven years old, students have already leaned a lot. Some of that learning is relevant to schooling and much of it is not. Children who come from families where parents are more highly educated, where there is reading material in the home, where siblings are doing well in school and where behavioural patterns match those in school are more likely to do well in school. Schools and school systems that have mainly these school-ready children are able to produce high test scores with less effort than those that have children with less academic skills acquired at home. One way to get at school quality differences within the same country or across countries is to compare how well pupils from families with the same relatively high levels of education do in different school, regional or national contexts.

A third drawback is that the tests (whether domestic or international) measure a set of academic skills but not other skills that may be just as useful in doing well economically and socially in the student's environment. For example, the TIMSS test does not measure an individual's persistence, networking skills or creativity. Educational attainment is a much better measure of persistence and perhaps networking skills, but not necessarily creativity.[2] But how do we measure whether a school system does well in developing creativity in its students? This would be a real challenge.

Despite these drawbacks, in the past five years, by using student achievement as a principal measure of school output, analysts have gained important insights into why children in some countries perform academically better than children of similar socio-economic background in others. International test score data and accompanying surveys of teachers, students and school directors have helped us reach these insights, but so have much more sophisticated data collection in the United States, Brazil and Mexico, for example, as well as studies of rural schools in Central America, classroom observations and school interviews in Brazil, Chile and Cuba, and educational experiments in India, Kenya and Latin American countries. These studies have taken us far beyond the production function analyses of the 1970s and 1980s, which (incorrectly) deemphasised the role of teacher skills and argued (correctly) for increasing non-teaching resources.

Recent research makes it possible to identify strategies that can work to improve schooling. Yet, they also show that this is not a simple task. There is no quick fix – no structural change, such as shifting from central to local administration, creating educational markets or simply publishing test scores, that induces educational improvement. The problem of quality is not lack of competition but lack of quality teachers and management. Whether private or public, schools cannot implement challenging curricula if teachers have low levels of subject knowledge and have little understanding of how to teach those curricula. Whether private or public, schools will not deliver a good product if management lacks instructional leadership and management skills. Who sets the standards in schools? Who defines quality and sets expectations for good teaching and student learning? If it is to be parents, as market advocates insist, then parents must be able to discern good from mediocre education – they have to be able to identify demanding curricula, challenging maths problems and good writing. Yet most parents seek the same education for their children that they had themselves (Anyon, 1983). In countries trying to reach goals set by EFA, a high percentage of parents have had little or no experience with education. How are they to be high standard setters?

Our comparative study of educational organisation, primary schools and third grade maths classrooms in Brazil, Chile and Cuba provided answers to some of these key questions (Carnoy, Gove and Marshall 2007). We found, first, that the socio-political context of schools has a significant impact on student outcomes and on the types of policy measures taken by governments to try to improve educational quality. The socio-political environment in which schooling takes place may be as important as individual families in affecting how much students learn.

The contrast between Cuba, Chile and Brazil brings this influence into sharp relief. Brazilian and Chilean social structures are much more unequal economically and ideologically than Cuba's. This has important implications for schooling, even if, in all three societies, education is viewed, ideologically, as the great social 'equalizer,' both transforming class structure into meritocracy, and binding pupils from different social classes to each other through the common experience of national education. In Cuba, this ideology is much closer to reality than in Chile or Brazil. The difference is especially evident in Brazil, where, even after a major financial reform, children in low-income regions go to schools with far fewer resources. Access to schooling is also still more limited than in Chile or Cuba. Thus, for Brazilian education even to *represent* itself as playing an equalising role, it has to get closer to Chilean educational reality, and Chilean educational reality continues to reproduce inequality when compared to Cuba's.

The socio-political environment also differentiates the way schools operate in the three countries. In Chile, which has had a national voucher plan since 1981 and where 46% of basic education students attend privately managed schools, the Ministry of Education develops the national curriculum, required in all schools – public and private – that accept funds from the government. However, the Ministry only uses indirect means to enforce the implementation of its curriculum. These indirect means consist of testing students every two years in the 4th, 8th and 10th grades, publishing the results for each school and monetarily rewarding the 25% of schools (primarily their teachers) that make the largest gains in each region. Principals of schools have the autonomy to take steps to improve their students' performance. Public school principals do not hire and fire teachers (municipalities do that), and public school teachers have tenure contracts, but private school operators have essentially full power to make staff decisions from year to year. For other matters besides curriculum and teacher hiring and firing, public school principals also have considerable leeway to experiment, mobilise other resources and be resourceful. On the whole, then, besides being required to teach the subject elements defined by the national curriculum, principals have a great deal of autonomy and decision-making power in Chile.

Whether they choose or know how to use this power to improve instruction is another matter, however. In both public and private schools in Chile, teachers have considerable autonomy in the classroom. Private school teachers can be fired for doing a bad job, but the principal of the school does not necessarily intervene to help them do a better job. There is little culture of the principal as instructional leader and there is a strong culture of classrooms as teachers' sanctuaries.

In Brazil, educational administration is highly decentralised to the state and municipal level, but only about ten per cent of students in basic education attend private primary school. The central government has developed curricular frameworks and approved textbooks. States and municipalities choose the curriculum they will use in locally run schools.

Like in Chile, school administrators have considerable autonomy in how they run the school, but teachers in public schools are hired and fired by state and municipal governments, not school administrations. The trend in Brazil is to put more emphasis on parent participation in the school (a consumer cooperative model of decision-making), on the theory that parents will pressure teachers to exert more effort. Since most parents have little information about how to measure teacher or school quality and do not have the opportunity to observe teachers teaching, parent participation has, not surprisingly, had little effect on instruction or administration in schools.

Cuba is very different from Brazil and Chile. Cuban society is tightly controlled and regimented. Individual choices exist but are narrower than in Chile or Brazil. The issue of choice is complex, since children in poor families in Brazil and Chile may have more 'choice' than, say, rural or low-income urban children in Cuba, but many of those choices are not positive – to work at odd jobs or hang out rather than going to school, to engage in illegal activities or not, or to join a gang or not.. The state in Cuba provides a rigid structure for family and youth choices, much as organised religion does in orthodox religious families and communities. In the Cuban restricted choice model, educational 'success' is part of that rigid structure: the state 'requires' children to be as successful in school as their ability permits.

Beyond the direct effect of socio-political structure on the context of schooling, the content knowledge and formation of teachers is much more tightly organised and controlled by the central state in Cuba than in either Brazil or Chile. Whereas in everyday life, this degree of state control impinges on individual freedom, in primary and secondary education, when combined with a commitment to high-quality outcomes and the drive for equity, the result is much greater quality control, more instructional leadership setting high standards in classrooms, and a well-defined and well-understood alignment between curriculum and teaching.

Comprehending how Cuba delivers such high-quality education at the primary and middle school levels in both urban and rural schools cannot be totally separated from Cuba's socio-political conditions, but there are many elements of the Cuban system that could be used to improve greatly schools in other countries. Figure 1.1 outlines the nature of the problem in the typical developing country educational system.[3]

In most countries, including Brazil and Chile, well-intentioned Ministry (or state or municipal) policies, such as curriculum frameworks, are weakly coupled (as shown in Figure 1.1) to actual school practice, because there is no supervisory/instructional assistance structure to ensure that the reforms are being implemented as anticipated in the reform programme. The 'educational market' in Chile, including a high degree of parent choice, many privately run schools and information for parents and schools provided by national testing, has apparently not improved teaching or raised average student performance. Further, teacher education is very important in influencing the nature of school practice, but Ministry policies are weakly coupled to teacher education, so university preparation of teachers does not necessarily conform to the improved capacity required by Ministry curricular reforms. Finally, school practice is important in influencing student outcomes, so the weak implementation of Ministry policy results in little improvement in school practice, hence results in little improvement of student outcomes.

Figure 1.1: Relations among components of the educational system in a typical developing-country educational system

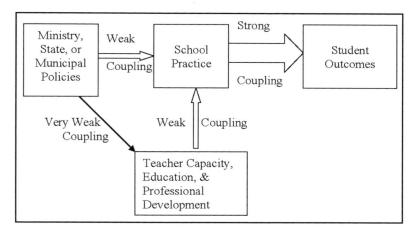

In Cuba, on the other hand, the links between the various components of this model are much stronger. Teachers have the advantage of higher levels of content knowledge thanks to the greater amount of content they learn in primary and secondary school. *The Cuban education system also has the enormous advantage of being able to recruit young people into teaching with relatively higher standing in their secondary school cohorts because markets do not determine Cuban salary struc-*

tures. The absence of market pricing of labour services creates problems elsewhere in the Cuban economy, but public services such as education and healthcare benefit from the artificially lower costs of high-quality labour.

Ministry reforms and the national curriculum in Cuba are tightly linked to teacher education and professional development because they are both run directly by the Ministry and focus on training teachers to deliver the national curriculum effectively. Beyond teachers' initial education, most teacher training takes place on the job, where new teachers are closely mentored by experienced teachers and school principals and vice-principals. These supervisors' job is *defined specifically as ensuring that teachers in their school are teaching the required demanding curriculum effectively, and that students are learning it.*

Our observations of teacher education, teacher supervision (on-the-job training) and school practice (including video tapes of 10 to 12 third-grade maths classrooms) in the three systems lead us to conclude that Cuba delivers more opportunity to learn to children in its schools than either Brazil and Chile, and does it mainly in four ways:

- The Cuban maths curriculum is more comprehensive and more theoretically integrated than Brazil's or Chile's. But Cuba's literacy curriculum does not differ appreciably from the other two.
- Cuban primary school teachers have a higher level of content knowledge, particularly in maths, thanks mainly to the higher levels of mathematics they attain in secondary school. This can be labled the 'virtuous circle' effect. Students are better prepared in subject matter knowledge, so the curriculum they teach when they become teachers can be more demanding.
- Teacher education in Cuba is strictly organised around teaching the required national curriculum. Pedagogical theory and child development are also an important part of the teacher education, but not at the expense of focusing on teaching teachers how to reach curricular objectives.
- Teachers are closely supervised in their classroom teaching by their principals and vice-principals. Every Cuban school is focused on instruction, and the primary responsibility of school administrators is to ensure that children in the school are

reaching clearly specified academic objectives.

These are precisely the elements that every country has to introduce in order to improve quality and ensure student completion of at least basic education. Countries need to improve teacher content knowledge, improve the level of the curriculum, make sure that teachers are taught to teach the high-level curriculum, and make sure that they implement the curriculum. In addition, of course, the educational system must expect that every child can succeed, and organise the system to ensure that every child *does* succeed.

The skeleton in the closet: Teacher absenteeism

An especially serious issue in teacher supervision and support concerns the actual number of days and hours per day school is in session. Parents who have never gone to school or who have not completed their primary education may not know much about the quality of teaching or the teacher's subject knowledge, but they do know that children don't learn much if the teacher is not in school. Many primary school children attend schools where teachers are often absent. Absenteeism is a major problem in many rural schools, but it is also a problem in urban areas. A Harvard University/World Bank team recently completed a study of teacher absenteeism in a number of countries, among them Bangladesh, Ecuador, India, Indonesia and Peru. The rate of absenteeism varies from country to country and among provinces within a country, but is often over 30% (Chaudhury et al 2006). Absenteeism is not necessarily the result of low teacher salaries. Teachers in Honduras, for example, are relatively well paid, but absenteeism is widespread (Bedi and Marshall 1999). High teacher absenteeism automatically means lower quality of education, and there is evidence that parents are more likely to keep their children home to work if they perceive schooling to be of low quality (Marshall 2003).

In a detailed study of Guatemalan rural schools, Jeffery Marshall (2003) observed classroom teaching, measured student performance gains and absences and estimated teachers' absences from school records in 58 isolated rural schools in three Guatemalan provinces. He also selected a sample of almost 1 100 pupils from the first grade rolls in these schools two years earlier and traced what happened to them between the first grade and the present. From these detailed data on attainment and achievement, Marshall was able to estimate correlates of attainment (probability of continuing on to a higher grade), student absence and achievement. The official school calendar requires 140 days of school, but Marshall's sample of schools averaged only 110 days. He found, using careful econometric analysis, that teacher absences (or rather the number of days school was in session) had a significant effect on all three of these dependent variables, particularly for boys. Indeed, an increase of ten days that a school was open (one standard deviation of school days) resulted in one-third of a standard deviation of test score increase for boys, and one-fifth of a standard deviation in attainment, again for boys, and somewhat less for girls. The shorter the distance to a middle school, the greater the attainment as well, suggesting that access to higher levels of schooling influences how long parents send their children to primary school.

Marshall's results provide the most detailed evidence that teacher absences are a signal that influence parents' valuation of schooling and that the high level of absences in Guatemalan rural schools affect student achievement and attainment, exactly the stated goals of EFA. The implications are clear: reducing teacher absences is key to achieving education for all. But how can education policy reduce absences? The World Bank is counting on community-based organisations paying teachers directly based on performance. Something similar is being used in Chad, where many teachers were being hired by communities anyway, so the Bank convinced the Ministry to pay many more teachers the same way, but using public funds. Colombia developed the *Escuela Nueva*, which focuses on bringing isolated rural teachers together in workshops one a month, using the workshops to help teachers improve their teaching and their schools. Evaluations of the *Escuela Nueva* show that it works well and is cost-effective (McEwan 1999). Cuba just makes sure that teachers show up, inculcating rural educators with a sense of mission in helping the lowest-income Cuban children have the same chances that are afforded to urban dwellers.

Whatever the response, solving teacher absences is fundamental to improving education. How well countries can respond to this problem is also indicative of countries' commitment to good education, and, for that matter, the professionalism of teachers. It is not as simple as it may seem. Absenteeism is a measure of system inefficiency and lack of supervision and control, but is also a measure of cynicism and corruption, neither of which is eliminated easily.

Evidence from randomised field trials

There is a strong argument that the only way to learn what strategies work to improve schooling is through randomised experiments that compare randomly assigned treatment and control groups. With randomised assignment, the effectiveness of programmes can be estimated without confronting the problem of selection bias (in which participants self-select into the treatment group).

Some of the interventions that have been tested with randomised evaluation studies have been: reducing the cost of education by paying low-income families to send their children to school, providing students with free school uniforms, providing students with scholarships based on test score performance, providing free school lunches, and deworming students who come to school. Interestingly, most of these interventions have a significant positive impact on student attendance at school, but not on their test score performance in school (Duflo 2006). The cost of these programmes per extra year of schooling attained by students is shown in Figure 1.2.

Figure 1.2: Cost-effectiveness of various school interventions (Duflo 2006)

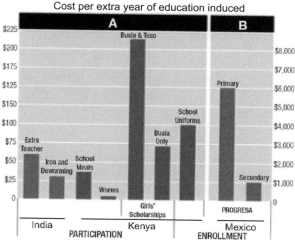

Other interventions, such as improving standard inputs – textbooks, flipcharts, etc. – and providing extra teachers, seem to have little effect on student achievement. The reason for this lack of progress appears to result from the negligible changes in pedagogy that accompany increases in these standard inputs.

There are however, more promising results from other programmes. A remedial education programme in India improved average test scores by 0,13 standard deviations (SDs) in the first year of the programme and 2,6 SDs in the second year. The lowest-scoring children improved their scores by 0,6 SDs.

One of the most controversial points of discussion is how to improve teacher attendance. As discussed above, this is a worldwide problem in developing countries, but is worse in some than others. Thus, interventions to improve teacher attendance could raise student learning considerably. One such intervention, reported by Duflo (2006), had a random sample of teachers in India photograph themselves and the class every day that they appeared in school. The photographs were electronically dated and the time recorded. The absence rate fell from 42% to 22% and test scores rose 0,17 standard deviations after a year of incentives. But other types of incentives in Kenya, based on headmaster reports or on test score gains rather than presence, did not have significant effects on student learning. Similarly, the results of community control programmes where communities monitor teacher absence have had disappointing results in relation to both teacher presence and student test scores (Duflo 2006).

Although these experiments are the best way to test the effectiveness of various educational interventions, they also have downsides, namely that they generally test an intervention in one environment at a time and under particular conditions. Scaling them up may also entail administrative difficulties that are not encountered by a small experiment. For example, administering teacher photographs as an incentive for reducing absence on a large scale could be very problematic. However, there is much to learn from experiments, and they should be carried out wherever possible to test interventions. Further, bad results need to be reported, as well as the ones that succeed.

A note on financing education and the quality/quantity strategy

In order to improve quality or expand access to successively higher levels of education for more students, nations need to find ways to increase the resources going to education. Some analysts have argued that there is a great deal of waste in the educational system, so that educational quality can be improved without more resources by finding more efficient ways to deliver education. The most prevalent among these arguments is that decentralisation and privatisation (a more market-oriented approach to educational delivery) increase educational output for the same level of resources.

Advocates argue that decentralisation shifts decision-making to those closer to the community and school, which in turn leads to decisions more responsive to local conditions and needs. They believe that it is a way to encourage greater community (parent) participation and financial support for schools. Opponents suggest that decentralising authority and responsibility may only shift the same old problems to levels of the system that are less well prepared to cope with them and that decentralising management invites corruption and inefficiency, or at least spreads it. They point out that since communities do not necessarily speak with a single voice, decentralisation has sometimes increased tension at the local level and allowed local majorities to create very unequal education for local minorities. Both advocates and opponents are probably right to some degree. Decentralisation can be a force for more relevance and allocative efficiency or can be an invitation to confusion and inefficiency. Which it is depends largely on the leadership at district, community and school level. Similarly, the efficiency of a centralised system depends on leadership at the central level. The wise use of resources to improve the quality of schooling will demand school managers who understand the elements of good instruction and who are not drawn off by pressures to spend money on show rather than substance. Unfortunately, this is precisely one of the scarcest resources in developing countries, and even in developed countries.

The more 'extreme' form of educational decentralisation is privatisation, which effectively moves control of resource allocation and pedagogical management down to school level. Proponents argue passionately that private education is more effective in bringing pupils to higher levels of achievement than public and is more cost-effective (see

Benveniste, Carnoy and Rothstein 2003 for a review of this literature). However, policy-makers have to be careful about claims that private schooling is the silver bullet that would improve the quality of primary and secondary education at relatively low public cost. Early studies of private education (Jimenez, Lockheed and Wattanawaha 1988) that purported to show higher effectiveness-cost ratios for private schools were later shown to have seriously underestimated private school costs (Tsang and Taoklam 1992), and the effectiveness estimates are not corrected for selection bias.

More recent and more careful studies analyzing Chile's national voucher plan and New Zealand's choice plan suggest that once socioeconomic background of students is accounted for, those in private schools do not achieve significantly higher than students in public schools (McEwan and Carnoy 2000; Fiske and Ladd 2000). One of the main arguments for privatisation is to allow for more parent choice and more competition among schools. The argument is that if parents can shift their children from one school to another, all schools will exert more effort to improve in order to attract more students (clients). Yet it is difficult to find evidence that competition has produced better schooling either in Chile (Hsieh and Urquiola 2001) or in the United States (Belfield and Levin 2002).

Furthermore, although parents who have educational choice for their children are more satisfied than parents who do not have choice, privatisation schemes at public expense appear to produce more *inequitable* distributions of students among schools. The Chilean case suggests strongly that to have an effective large-scale private school system, a country needs the same teacher and managerial capacity in education as required to have an effective public school system. The Chileans claim that subsidising private schools and allowing private schools to charge tuition has enabled the government to raise considerable private funds and save public resources. But the bottom line is that privatisation has not improved the quality of education (Chilean test scores have not risen over time) and Chile does no better on international tests than other large Latin American countries, such as Mexico, with relatively small proportions of pupils in privately run schools.

Thus, the motives for decentralisation or privatisation are not necessarily related to improving education. It is often undertaken to increase community financial contribution as a means of easing the financial burden on central government. No empirical evidence exists that decentralised school systems are more effective or efficient than centralised systems. Further, there is relatively little evidence to suggest that decentralising an education system changes the experience of children in classrooms. This is not to suggest that decentralisation is not a desirable goal, but only to suggest it may not address education outcomes. Indeed, as we suggest below, many countries have had *de facto decentralization* for a long time owing to weak management at the central level or poor communication across all levels. In these settings, local schools have always had to rely on their communities to provide what central government has been unwilling or unable to provide, and most teachers are unsupervised in their classrooms and receive almost no technical support.

Those who argue for decentralisation also argue for central state 'regulation' or monitoring through student testing – standard setting, as it were. But nations that regularly test all students in all grades, such as the US or Chile, have found that although schools pay attention to student test scores, they cannot be counted on to improve teaching and student outcomes unless there are sanctions for not doing so (Carnoy and Loeb 2003). Even then, the results may be uneven unless the state takes effective action to increase teacher and managerial capacity to change what goes on in classrooms. If states are already willing and able to identify problem schools and teachers and help them improve, why bother to decentralise and privatise?

The bottom line is that decentralisation of management can work well in countries where there is already sufficient capacity at the local level to allocate resources efficiently and to produce effective education. Ironically, it is precisely in those countries with good management at the central level that we can expect to find more capacity at the local level. The advantage of schools well run locally is that they are indeed rooted in the community and can be flexible to community needs as well as providing a sound basic education. The advantage of a well-run centralised system is that it can provide effective schools across socio-economic strata, reducing the negative consequences of unequal management capacity in different regions and localities.

Nevertheless, the argument that educational choice may induce greater willingness on the part of parents to contribute considerable amounts privately to schooling is an important one. If a country is willing to sustain greater inequality of resources among schools attended by families with different capacities to pay, this is a reasonable solution to raising more resources for schools in countries with inefficient tax collection systems. Alternatively, public financing can be allocated to schools inversely to the social class of students in the school – lower-income students could receive higher amounts per student of public money, whereas schools with higher-income students would have to raise more money privately. Chile is considering such an inverse voucher.

Another way to play this financial card is to increase the amount of private financing required at increasingly higher levels of schooling, with an increasing use of larger public vouchers or full scholarships for low-income students. The most obvious level at which to apply this is at the university level, generally attended by a higher fraction of higher social class students than at the primary and secondary level. The United States has applied this system most successfully. There is a great deal of higher education choice in the US, generally high tuition, and considerable financial aid based on need. With a considerable fraction of higher education costs borne privately by students, even at public universities, this frees up states to spend more at the primary and secondary level. Other countries such as Korea and Chile have an even higher fraction of university spending financed directly by private contributions.

With more private financing at the university level, the role of the public sector should shift from the sole funder of universities to regulating and ensuring equity in higher education. Universities are the top of educational systems and implicitly drive standards at lower levels of schooling. But universities in most countries are generally accountable only to themselves, despite receiving public funding. A number of German states have instituted a system of accountability that determines how much funding universities get. There is a move in the OECD to evaluate university faculties in various countries to determine how much students are learning. By combining increased accountability for public funding with increased scholarships for needy students, the public sector could increase efficiency and equity in universities. By making accountability results available to the public, families would be more willing to pay to send their children to more effective than to less effective higher education institutions.

Conclusions

All this suggests that there is no quick fix for educational quality in developing countries. This raises a crucial issue: can countries 'afford' to focus their efforts on raising achievement outcomes at each level of schooling? Is such an effort the best strategy to raising the knowledge base in the labour force and building a more informed populace?

Historically, nations have not been successful in raising the average achievement of students in, say, the 8th grade, as we discussed above. In case the 1970 to 1994 period is too short to convince the reader that average test scores have not increased (or declined) much over time, look at the Iowa Test of Basic Skills, applied annually to 8th graders in the state of Iowa since 1935. Average scores increased somewhat until the 1960s, then declined, then increased slightly and, in the 1990s, began to decline again. Over the whole period, scores fell somewhat (Rothstein 1998).

Based on careful studies of student performance, most researchers are now concluding that student performance at a given level of schooling will not improve unless a more demanding curriculum is taught to students by teachers with reasonably high levels of subject matter knowledge well trained to teach that curriculum and believing that every student is capable of learning it. In order to ensure that teachers are carrying out this mandate, a supervision system has to be in place that helps teachers reach high levels of competence in their practice and that ensures they show up regularly to actually teach the curriculum.

Realistically, improving teacher content knowledge and making them effective pedagogues, including the required supervision and assistance by skilled supervisors, is bound to be expensive. It implies a massive investment in capacity, either by raising educators' starting salaries substantially to recruit a new brand of educator (Chile has implemented large salary increases in the past seven years with positive effects on attracting better high school graduates to teachers' colleges) or by making large investments and totally reforming teacher education. This still leaves the existing teacher corps, which would have to take intensive maths and language courses and learn to teach a more demanding curriculum. Again, the system would have to invest heavily in developing the supervision skills among current administrators or selecting and paying the best teachers higher salaries to be supervisors/assistors.

In the long run, increasing student learning significantly in primary and secondary school would have a high payoff, mainly in terms of producing a whole new generation of teachers with greater subject knowledge, which would in turn ratchet up the next generation of students' performance. This is expensive, though, and should be recognised as such.

It turns out that in practice, countries and communities do not raise average knowledge in their societies by increasing average achievement levels at each level of schooling. The main path that countries have taken historically to higher average achievement is to increase average educational attainment. Even as average achievement has not increased in countries, the average level of education attained has risen dramatically worldwide.

A primary school graduate in, say, India is much more likely to know how to add, subtract and multiply and to be able to read than an adult with two or three years of primary school. A secondary school graduate knows more mathematics and has better language skills than a primary graduate. It may seem strange that keeping an average young person in school for an additional three years is cheaper than, say, doubling the amount that a child learns in three years of schooling, but apparently that is the case. Our analysis suggests why it probably *is* the case. Raising teacher skills and improving classroom practices apparently enables some nations, such as Korea, to teach children of a similar social class background as much mathematics in six years of primary school as other countries, such as South Africa or Chile, are able to teach them in eight. But it is, we would argue, far less expensive for South Africa or Chile to bring even middle class children to a 6th grade level of Korean knowledge by keeping them in school for eight years than to try to improve their primary education to a Korean level.

At the same time, it appears that raising student achievement and educational quality in general for low-income students is much more feasible technically and financially than raising the quality of an 'average' school. Marshall's analysis of the effect of significantly increasing the number of days of schooling in rural areas provides a clear example of high payoff to a quality improvement investment that increases both student achievement and attainment. Yet, even in this case, an important complement to reducing teacher absenteeism is increasing access for rural students to lower secondary schools. This second strategy, which focuses directly on increasing the number of years that rural children have available to go to school, sends an important signal to parents that investing more of their children's time in primary school gives them a shot at secondary education, and perhaps a ticket to a better job.

In most countries – even developed ones – it is the bottom of the educational distribution that is of most concern, hence raising quality of education for low-income groups does make sense. Some countries have such low levels of education, however, that simply increasing the average number of years of education attained may still be the most efficient strategy to follow. This may require a large investment, mainly in additional classrooms and teachers, but that in and of itself could also be a major factor in raising the quality of schooling. 'Traditional' approaches to quality, such as reducing first grade class sizes from 110 to 35 and adding inexpensive textbooks and reading materials for all children, still have a lot going for them when conditions are so poor in school that even these fundamentals are missing. At the same time, policy-makers should not forget that strategies aimed at improving quality, increased access, and remediation at university level could have an important impact on the quality of primary and particularly secondary education. At a minimum, improving the quality of higher education for teachers could translate into better teaching at lower levels of schooling.

References

Anyon, J. (1983) Social class and the hidden curriculum of work. In Giroux, H and Purpel, D (eds). *The Hidden Curriculum and Moral Education: Deception or Discovery?* Berkeley, CA: McCutchan Publishing Corporation, 143-167.

Bedi, AS and Marshall, JH. (1999) School attendance and student achievement: Evidence from rural Honduras. *Economic Development and Cultural Change* 47: 657-682.

Belfield, C and Levin, HM. (2002) *The Effects of Competition on Educa-*

tional Outcomes: A Review of US Evidence. New York: National Center for the Study of Privatization.

Benveniste, L, Carnoy, M and Rothstein, R. (2003) *All Else Equal.* New York: Routledge.

Carnoy, M. (1972) The political economy of education. In LaBelle, T (ed.). *Education and Development in Latin America and the Caribbean.* Los Angeles, CA: UCLA Latin American Center.

Carnoy, M. (1993) *The Case for Basic Education.* New York: UNICEF.

Carnoy, M. (1994) *Faded Dreams.* New York: Cambridge University Press.

Carnoy, M. (1995) Rates of return to education. In Carnoy, M. (ed.). *The International Encyclopedia of the Economics of Education.* Oxford, UK: Pergamon.

Carnoy, M. (2000) *Sustaining the New Economy.* Cambridge, MA: Harvard University Press.

Carnoy, M and DeAngelis, K. (2000) *Does 'ability' influence individual earnings, and if so, by how much?* Stanford University School of Education (mimeo).

Carnoy, M, Cosse, G, Cox, C, and Martinez, E. (2003) *Las Lecciones de la Reforma Educativa en el Cono Sur Latinoamericano: Un Estudio Comparado de Argentina, Chile y Uruguay en los Noventa.* Buenos Aires: CRESUR.

Carnoy, M and Loeb, S. (2003) Does external accountability affect student outcomes? A cross-state analysis. *Educational Evaluation and Policy Analysis,* 24(4): 305-331.

Carnoy, M and Marshall, JH. (2003) *Comparing Cuban Academic Performance with the Rest of Latin America: A Socio-Political Context Approach.* Stanford University School of Education (mimeo).

Carnoy, M, Gove, A and Marshall, JH. (2007) *Why Do Students Achieve More in Some Countries than Others? A Comparative Study of Brazil, Chile, and Cuba.* Palo Alto, CA: Stanford University Press (in press).

Chaudhury, N, Hammer, J, Kremer, M, Muralidharan, K and Rogers, FH. (2006) Missing in action: Teacher and health worker absence in developing countries. *Journal of Economic Perspectives* 20(1): 91-116.

Duflo, E. (2006) Evaluation education policy: Lessons from randomized evaluations. Presentation at the International Conference on Economics of Education, University of Burgundy, Dijon, France, 21-23 June.

EFA (Education For All). (2005) *Global Monitoring Report – The quality imperative.* Paris: UNESCO.

Fiske, E and Ladd, H. (2000) *When Schools Compete: A Cautionary Tale.* Washington, DC: Brookings Institution.

Hanushek, E and Kimko, D. (2000) Schooling, labor force quality, and the growth of nations. *American Economic Review*, 90(5): 1184-1208.

Hanushek, E and Wößmann, L. (2006) *The Role of School Improvement in Economic Development*. Cambridge, MA: National Bureau of Economic Research.

Hsieh, CT and Urquiola, M. (2002) *When school compete, how do they compete? An assessment of Chile's nationwide voucher program*. Occasional Paper No. 43. New York: National Center for the Study of Privatization.

Jimenez, E, Lockheed, M and Wattanawaha, N. (1988) The relative efficiency of public and private schools: The case of Thailand. *The World Bank Economic Review*, 2(2): 139-164.

McEwan, PJ. (1999) Evaluating rural education reform: The case of Colombia's *Escuela Nueva* program. *La Educación*, 132-133: 35-56.

McEwan, P and Carnoy, M. (2000) The effectiveness and efficiency of private schools in Chile's voucher system. *Educational Evaluation and Policy Analysis*, 22(3) (Fall): 213-239.

Marshall, JH. (2003) *If You Build It Will They Come?* Stanford University School of Education (mimeo).

Mingat A and Tan, JP. (1996) *The full social returns to education*. Human Capital Working Papers. Washington DC: World Bank.

Pritchett, L. (2003) Educational Quality and Costs: A Big Puzzle and Five Possible Pieces. Article at, referenced 9 October 2007.

Rothstein, R. (1998) *The Way We Were? Myths and Realities of America's Student Achievement*. New York: Century Foundation Press.

Tsang, M. and Taoklam, W. (1992) Comparing the costs of public and private primary education in Thailand. *International Journal of Education and Development*, 12(3): 177-190.

Welmond, M. (2002) Teacher identity in the Republic of Benin. *Comparative Education Review*, 46: 37-65.

Portions of this chapter are drawn from a 2004 report to UNESCO, Paris, on the EFA initiatives.

[1] Early theoretical work by Carnoy (1972) and recent research findings (Carnoy 1995 and Mingat and Tan 1996) on the levels of return to education suggest that (a) for low-income countries, primary education is the best investment, (b) for middle-income countries, secondary education yields the highest social returns, and (c) for higher-income countries, tertiary education yields the highest returns. Mingat and Tan's research accounts for externalities, not typically taken into account, that benefit society, e.g. the increased productivity of educated workers

may increase the productivity of co-workers, and a rise in the general education of the labour force may increase the potential for innovations and adaptations leading to more long-term efficiencies in the workplace. But even without counting externalities, the pattern of rates of return over time as education expands and the economy develops, requiring increasing proportions of higher educated workers to produce increasingly sophisticated goods and services, shifts toward higher payoffs to higher levels of education.

[2] Colleges in the United States that take the time to examine a broader range of indicators in their applicants' dossiers than just test scores and grades generally seem to end up with a more diverse, interesting, and successful student body than those that put greater emphasis on test results. However, even the colleges that follow this more eclectic approach demand relatively high scores and good grades.

[3] This is a schematic of educational delivery by the state, and consciously does not include the influence of parents, which, to various degrees, affects Ministry policies, school practice and student outcomes. The figure is meant to represent the main variables affecting outcomes *controlling for* parent socio-economic background. Student outcomes include not only achievement scores, but also student attendance, student promotion and student attainment.

Aid agency support for education: Gaps between intention and action

Christopher COLCLOUGH

Strong commitments were made by the Millennium Declaration, in 2000, to achieve universal primary enrolment, gender equality and women's empowerment as part of a set of policies to halve the incidence of poverty by 2015. The international aid community played a central role in this process. This chapter asks whether the aid mechanisms for achieving these goals are in place and whether the processes of international monitoring and accountability that have been established are adequate for the task.

A brief history of the education goals

The global commitment to secure universal access and gender equality in education has been built, over the past 35 years, on the basis of two sets of initiatives. Firstly, a series of international treaties has been adopted and ratified by the great majority of countries that require states to make education universally available and to pursue educational policies that do not discriminate on the grounds of gender.[1]

Even though consensus on achieving these objectives appears to exist, the fact that many states have ratified these treaties does not imply that the rights and obligations they require will be observed. To help secure such observance, governments are expected to make regular reports in order to allow the relevant UN treaty organisations to be informed of progress made. In fact, however, such reports have typically not been lodged by about one third of the ratifying states (Tomasevski 2003). This prevents reliable international assessments of progress being made and, because they can remain unremarked, the treaty obligations are widely ignored in many of such cases.

31

Recognising this patchy implementation, a second set of initiatives has comprised a series of international declarations issued under the auspices of the United Nations. These have followed from the World Conferences on Education for All (1990), on Human Rights (1993), on Population and Development (1994), on Women (1995) and on Social Development (1995) and provide separate commitments on the part of all signatories to provide universal access to schooling and to protect and promote the rights of women in education and throughout society.[2]

A number of these commitments were brought together by the Development Assistance Committee (DAC) of the OECD in May 1996 (OECD DAC 1996), as part of a broader attempt to establish accepted targets for international development. The DAC adopted a new development strategy for global progress that embraced many of the development goals – including those for education and for gender equality – that had emerged from the UN summits earlier in the decade. A limited number of indicators were proposed for use as monitoring instruments, so as to assess progress towards the goals. Subsequently, many donors incorporated these principles into their aid policies, and many also began to see the DAC International Development Targets (IDTs) as key goals to inform their own aid allocations and to judge national development performance.

At its July 1999 meeting, the UN Economic and Social Council adopted a resolution to develop indicators on means of implementing the conference goals and to mobilise resources in support of national statistical capacity-building. The process was further formalised at the 2000 UN Millennium Summit, when world leaders from rich and poor countries alike committed themselves – at the highest political levels – to a set of eight time-bound targets that, when achieved, were expected to halve poverty worldwide by 2015. The first seven of these goals gave commitments to cut the incidence of poverty and hunger, get every child into school, empower women, reduce child mortality, improve maternal health, combat HIV/AIDS, malaria and other diseases, and ensure environmental sustainability. The eighth goal recognised that eradicating poverty worldwide could be achieved only through a global partnership for development: in order for poor countries to achieve the first seven goals, it would be absolutely critical that wealthier countries delivered on their end of the bargain – more and more effective aid, more sustainable debt relief and fairer trade rules – throughout the 15-year period to 2015.

The commitments for education were further extended at the World Education Forum, held in Senegal in 2000, to review the global commitments for educational progress. This meeting agreed on six 'Education for All' goals, which were considered to be essential, attainable and affordable. The 'Dakar Framework for Action', promulgated by the Forum, declared that by 2015 all children of primary-school age would participate in free schooling of acceptable quality, that adult illiteracy would be halved, that progress would be made in providing early childhood care and education, and that learning opportunities for the youth and adults and all aspects of education quality would be improved. One of these 'Dakar' goals also committed all nations to 'eliminating gender disparities in primary and secondary education by 2005, and achieving gender equality in education by 2015, with a focus on ensuring girls' full and equal access to and achievement in basic education of good quality' (UNESCO 2000b: paragraph 7).

It is worth noting that, by contrast, the third Millennium Development Goal, which commits signatories to 'promote gender equality and empower women', uses a more generalised wording, which extends well beyond the framework of education. However, the operational target by which this goal will be achieved and monitored is to 'eliminate gender disparity in primary and secondary education, preferably by 2005, and to all levels of education no later than 2015' (UN 2001, Resolution A/56/326). This target is often misleadingly taken as being synonymous with the gender goal itself, whereas it was, at the time, judged to be simply the main way in which indicators for equality and empowerment could be monitored.[3]

Are the goals consistent and achievable?[4]

Both the Dakar gender goal and the MDG gender target aimed to achieve parity in primary and secondary enrolments by 2005. Yet at the time these goals were agreed, in 2000, it was already clear that that target could not be met. In order to do so, over the intervening five years, large numbers of out-of-school girls would have needed to enrol in (or rejoin) classes at levels well beyond primary grade 1. Such 'mid-career' enrolment would have been extensively required if secondary enrolment parity were to have been achieved within a five-year period, at least in those many school systems in which male pupils significantly outnumbered girls at all grade levels. This kind of enrolment behaviour would have been unsustainable over the medium term and, in most countries, it would be infeasible in the first place.

Table 2.1 Successive international development goals for education

Date	Event	Goal	Target date
1990	WCEFA	UPE	2000
1995	FWCW	Primary enrolment parity	2000
1995	WSSD	Prim/sec enrolment parity	2005
2000	WEF	UPE	2015
		Prim/sec enrolment parity	2005
		Gender equality in education	2015
2000	UN Summit	UPE	2015
		Prim/sec enrolment parity	2005
		All levels enrolment parity	2015

Note: Acronyms represent the following events:
WCEFA – World Conference on Education for All, Jomtien, Thailand
FECW – First World Conference on Women, Beijing, China
WSSD – World Summit for Social Development, Copenhagen, Denmark
WEF – World Education Forum, Dakar, Senegal
UN Summit – UN Millennium Summit, New York, USA.

It is not clear why the international community has made a habit of setting unrealistic target dates for the achievement of its educational goals. From Table 2.1, it can be seen that each of the targets set for 2000 or 2005 envisaged an impossibly rapid reform agenda: achieving universal primary education over ten years from 1990, or gender parity of enrolments over five years from 1995 or from 2000 were infeasible tasks. It had, for example, taken 30 years for primary enrolments in developing countries to increase from half to three-quarters of all children of primary-school age by 1990. Enrolments would have had to double in sub-Saharan Africa, and to triple in many countries in the region, if all children were to be enrolled by the century's end (see Colclough with Lewin 1993: Table 1.3 and p.214). Similarly, it had taken almost two decades for female enrolments to increase from 79% to 84% of those of males by the late 1990s (see Colclough, Al-Samarrai, Rose and Tembon, 2003: Table 2.2). A move to parity over a five-year period was near impossible in the face of these historical trends. Thus, it was predictable that both the enrolment and the gender goals would not be achieved within the time frames chosen. Only those set for 2015 appeared to allow sufficient time to be achievable, provided that concerted national and international action in support of the goals were sustained over the 15-year period. It could, of course, be argued that failure to achieve the first of the Millennium Development Goals (MDGs), which occurred in 2005, would provide an additional incentive to marshal further support and try harder, and that deliberate over-optimism was thus built into the goal-setting process. Yet such intentional subtlety seemed, in the event, denied by the nature of the discussions at the UN Special Assembly on the Millennium Goals, held in New York in September 2005. These scarcely alluded to the world's failure to achieve the gender target in that year – preferring, instead, to concentrate attention on the ways and means of reaching those set for 2015.

The targets associated with the MDGs appear straightforward, but their achievement is often highly complex and context-specific. Yet simple targets are often (wrongly) taken to require the adoption of simple policy measures in response. For example, much of the aid debate has tended to revolve around the amount of resources required to achieve the MDGs. Plugging the financial gaps – as illustrated by much of the post-Gleaneagles (2005) political debate – has been taken to be the main challenge. Yet many of the demand-side constraints to achieving universal enrolment (as opposed to universal access and provision) need a much more subtle approach to diagnosis and policy reform than is often credited. For example, in circumstances where around 100 countries with low enrolments are still charging fees to attend primary schooling, the mere building of more schools is unlikely to result in easy or rapid increases in enrolment. Additional finance in these cases is of course required – but its use would be better directed towards reducing the direct costs of school attendance by abolishing fees, and even by putting more money, directly or indirectly, into the pockets of households, rather than directing it towards increasing the supply of school places.[5]

The differences between the MDG and Dakar wording imply that the question of what is meant by equality is central to an assessment of whether or not it can be achieved. The MDG target mentions only the need to achieve enrolment parity – i.e. equal numbers (or proportions) of boys and girls attending school, college or university. This notion of parity is a quantitative, static concept. However, when tracked over time a more dynamic indicator of change can be constructed. If progress towards gender parity in enrolments suggests a weakening of the structures that privilege men in society, it represents a step towards achieving equality in a broader sense. Nevertheless, making progress towards parity could also be consistent with enrolment declines for boys, girls or both being recorded. This in fact happened during the 1990s in Africa, where the impact of recession and adjustment brought a reduction of primary school enrolments in many countries – more strongly so for boys than for girls (see Colclough et al. 2003: 29-30; Rose 1995). Here, then, an apparent move towards gender parity was secured in a highly undesirable way. The demonstration of progress towards parity thus needs to take account of the absolute as well as the relative levels of educational attainment and achievement: it is not merely the quantitative balances themselves that are of importance, but also the processes by which they are secured.

The wording of the Dakar goal directly takes on the more ambitious agenda of achieving gender equality in education. Although definitions vary, full equality would seem to require the achievement of equality of opportunities to access education, of equality in learning processes whilst at school, of equality of outcomes – such that learning achievements would not differ by gender – and, finally, of equality of external results – such that job opportunities and earnings for men and women with similar qualifications would be equal. These are demanding conditions, the details of which fall outside the territory of this chapter (for discussion of these issues see UNESCO 2003, chapters 3 and 4). For present purposes, however, we should note that the use of the gender parity indicator alone provides an inadequate proxy for the achievement of equality in education in this broader sense. Identifying the true nature of the global agenda is thus not straightforward. Even achieving enrolment parity will require social and economic changes that go beyond the purview of Ministers of Education. Achieving equality in education is, of course, a much more ambitious objective.

The extent to which either of these goals can be achieved in poor states is dependent, usually, upon an approach to policy reform that is deeply rooted, and that embraces a sophisticated understanding of the causes of existing inequalities. There has, since the early 1970s, been a bifurcation between descriptive or developmentalist work on gender issues (often referred to as 'women in development' (WID) approaches) and more structural and analytic ('gender and development' – GAD) approaches to understanding discrimination and female subordination. The language of international policy has traditionally tended towards the former. Although the statement risks caricature, many international documents have presupposed that if elite groups could be shown that the continued propagation of inequality was against the interests not only of the excluded groups, but of national development more generally, policies would change to remedy the earlier oversight. Arguably the vocabularies of both the MDGs and the Dakar goals are in this tradition. These education goals urge the world to move towards equality by achieving parity of enrolments – as though this can be done simply by moving easily accessible policy levers, bringing outcomes that will have positive or neutral, rather than negative, effects for sections of important elite groups.

On the other hand, the ways in which the international system has analysed prospects for their better attainment have been more subtle than the initial formulation of the goals seemed to imply. The analysis of the 2003/4 EFA Global Monitoring Report (UNESCO 2003) and of the MDG Task Force 3 Report (UN Millennium Project 2005), both of which highlight the themes of gender and education, are in the GAD rather than the WID traditions, even though the latter tends to become dominant when it comes to proposing practical ways forward for policy (see Unterhalter 2005: 23-24). Although the need for profound social and economic change as a means to achieve gender equality is a recurring theme of these analyses, for pragmatic reasons many of their practical proposals have to entertain a more gradualist approach to reform.

Questions of implementation
Even if adequate policy change were indeed within reach, how could countries be held to their promises? If national governments choose to ignore the commitments that they have publicly espoused there is no easy sanction available to the international community to impose a change in their behaviour. As suggested earlier, adding the political

commitments made in UN Declarations to the legal undertakings embedded in UN human rights treaties may be expected to increase the likelihood that governments will take their own pledges seriously. But it does not guarantee that that will be so, as the continued low enrolments and substantial inequality between male and female school enrolments in more than 90 countries demonstrates (the data are shown in UNESCO 2005: 72). There are two main ways in which the international community can bring pressure to bear: firstly, periodic reporting of progress towards the EFA goals at the national level provides some accountability of governments and international agencies for actions taken or missed. Secondly, negotiated partnership arrangements – notably between governments and international agencies via the international aid process – provide a means of leverage to secure 'better' education policies in exchange for the provision of financial and technical aid resources over the medium term. In what follows we assess the effectiveness of present international practice along each of these dimensions.

Although both of these instruments may, even in principle, have only limited power to influence action, there is an important question as to whether the established machinery is best suited to the tasks in hand. In that regard, UNESCO was assigned a central role by the World Education Forum. The organisation was mandated to take the lead in sustaining international support for EFA and to promote better global coordination of such efforts. Although it has had some success as regards informing the global debate and providing a key means of increasing the accountability of national and international EFA actors, it has been less clearly successful in leading and coordinating increased international support for EFA. This is partly because it is difficult for an agency that does not itself have access to significant resources to influence the decisions of those who do have such access and to mobilise new aid monies for EFA.

Two developments attended UNESCO's enhanced role. First the Director-General convened annually (from 2001) a small and flexible 'High Level Group' that would meet to discuss detailed progress towards EFA and to design strategies for its improvement. The Group has comprised Ministers of Education or their representatives from some 10 to 15 countries, bilateral and multilateral development agencies (usually represented by the heads of their education division), academic commentators, and directors of a set of international and national NGOs that are active in education or judged to be articulate in matters of educational aid and policy. The membership of the Group has changed somewhat – mainly because of differences in the mix of countries represented – from year to year. It issues a communiqué at the end of the meeting, which is variously reported by the international press. The intention was that the content of this document would influence national and international educational policy and that it would inform international public opinion on questions of 'education for all'.

The second development was the establishment of a new annual publication – an EFA Global Monitoring Report (GMR) – that would provide an independent and high-quality assessment of the world's progress towards EFA and that would directly inform the deliberations of the High Level Group. This publication has been produced annually since 2002 by a team that is based in UNESCO but remains independent of it in terms of its professional stance and editorial policy. The report has been well resourced by a group of bilateral agencies. It provides a global statistical overview both of education systems, in considerable detail, and of aid to education, drawing upon the resources of the UNESCO Institute of Statistics in Montreal, and of the OECD DAC database in Paris. It also analyses key issues and challenges for education and aid policies, informed by a large body of research commissioned and/or synthesised by the report team. Annual issues since 2002 have covered financing EFA, gender equality, the quality of education, literacy, and early childhood care and education respectively. The EFA GMR has achieved wide international currency and influence. A recent evaluation of the first three reports, commissioned by the international community, finds that it is widely judged to be 'a high quality, authoritative document that has become a flagship for UNESCO' (Universalia 2006: 8). It has improved both the flow of information and the quality of analysis of the issues, so that the policy-making process at the international level is better-informed than before.

On the other hand, its influence upon opinion and policy has been neither linear nor uncontentious. As an example of this it is worth considering the impact of the Education for All Development Index (EDI), which was first published in the 2003/4 GMR and has subsequently been updated annually (see UNESCO 2003: 284-292 and subsequent volumes in the series). This index aims to provide a summary statistic that indicates the progress countries are making towards EFA in such a way that they can be compared and ranked, one with another. Its constituents reflect four of the six Dakar goals, one indicator being included as a proxy measure for each of them.[6] Rather like the Human Development Index, which is not necessarily strongly correlated with the usual indicators of development success, the EDI reveals that some relatively well-off and successful countries (such as South Africa, Saudi Arabia and Guatemala) are in fact strongly lagging on EFA-progress measures, whereas some low-income countries (such as Cuba, Guyana and Tajikistan) have very high EDI scores. These kinds of comparison serve to show that many of the countries with low levels of educational provision could – given greater political commitment – sharply improve their relative positions. In other words, much more could be done by these countries to live up to their agreed EFA commitments.

There is, almost always, a range of technical issues to overcome in the construction of an index. For example, in the case of the UNDP's Human Development Index, there is a problem as to how to add together, or even compare the relative importance of, its selected constituents – life expectancy at birth, the adult literacy rate, the gross enrolment ratio, and GDP per capita – within the same index. Even where measurement problems do not impose incommensurability, there is a real question as to how the different elements in an index should be weighted. In that case, value judgements are inescapable, which can affect national index values and country rankings.[7] However, in the case of the EDI, the technical problems are relatively absent – all constituents of the index can be expressed in percentages and each of them provides a reasonably direct proxy measure for the relevant Dakar goal. Moreover, since the Dakar Framework document does not assign greater importance to the achievement of some goals than others, there is no obvious need to weight any of the constituents of the index with values other than unity. Thus the index is calculated as a simple average of the percentage values for each of the four indicators of progress towards EFA.

Notwithstanding its relatively uncomplicated design, the index at first proved controversial, mainly because it provided a transparent instrument for making simple comparisons and, sometimes, for delivering unpalatable messages. Representatives of some countries with low values for the EDI objected to its methods of calculation and to the reliability of the data it utilised. They pointed to the time lag of some two or three years between the collection of the data and their publication internationally, thereby implying that the reliability, or currency, of the messages they contained could be questioned. This aspect of securing accountability proved to be one of the more contentious aspects of the GMR's impact.

However, a number of countries accepted the power of the index and began to use it as a criterion for their own success: the new Indian administration, for example, announced at the High Level Group meeting in Brasilia in November 2004 that they had adopted a target of India being in the top half of the index by 2010. Furthermore, the press in most countries seized on the index as an excellent means of producing attention-grabbing copy, and it allowed a straightforward way for lobbyists to call government ministers to account for their country's present position on EFA and to commit themselves to improving it.

The claim that the data were too old to be dependable was not a tactic used only by those developing countries that were embarrassed by their position in the national rank order of EFA progress. It was also used by some of the international agencies that found themselves compared unfavourably with others that were allocating more substantial resources to securing EFA objectives (usually via support to basic education and primary schooling). Such agency representatives typically argued that their policies had changed and that data for the most recent year (rather than the preceding one) would show that their aid programmes were, in fact, clearly focused on the achievement of EFA objectives. The fact that the discussion topics at the HLG were only rarely formally revisited the following year meant that the subject – and the particular nature of the protest – might escape re-inspection when the data had become available.[8]

This suggests a more fundamental flaw with recent processes of international coordination of EFA. The machinery, such as it is, is mainly contingent. The High Level Group itself has had little formal status and its outcome has not extended beyond the issuing of a communiqué that has no formal status on the international stage. Although it may achieve some coverage in the international press, its proposals for action do not get translated upwards either within the UN bureaucracy or in a parallel international political process. The impact of the communiqué has not generally been monitored, nor even formally revisited, in successive HLG meetings. The influence of its messages has been determined more by the quality of the Global Monitoring Report document, and by the extent of its dissemination, than by the formal discussions at the High Level Group meetings.

A second example of the presence of flaws in the international coordination of EFA lies in the recent history of donor 'pledging' as a means to achieve the MDGs, which has often occurred without securing the appropriate institutional means for delivering on their commitments. By 2005, donor countries had made significant promises for increased aid and debt relief. They promised to increase overall development assistance by around two-thirds (including a doubling of aid to Africa) and they agreed to cancel all the debt owed by the world's poorest countries to the World Bank, the IMF and the African Development Bank. They did not, however, make any particular commitments on education. Such sectoral allocations could have been discussed in September 2005 at the World Summit convened by the UN and/or at the World Bank/International Monetary Fund meetings that followed a few weeks later. But the UN summit barely managed to eke out a general document, merely reaffirming the global commitment to education for all, without providing any guidance as to the likely sectoral allocations of the additional monies pledged.

For education, this failure to secure agreement was a lost opportunity. Recent work commissioned by British government agencies has shown that the total additional aid needed to achieve the goals of universal primary education and gender parity will be approximately $10 billion per year over the decade to 2015. *Total* aid to basic education currently is scarcely more than one quarter of that amount, at around $2,7 billion per year (UNESCO 2006: 346). The amount of additional investment needed would account for more than 20% of the total additional aid commitments agreed at the G8 summit at Gleneagles and would, if forthcoming, help to set the majority of countries back on track to achieving the education goals.

There are, of course, major practical constraints preventing individual bilateral agencies from scaling up their programmes of assistance as rapidly as the above financing magnitudes would seem to require. However, in that context, donors have largely failed to take advantage of the major existing multilateral mechanism for channelling aid to education – the 'Fast Track Initiative' (FTI). One of the most powerful (and most frequently quoted) commitments made at the Dakar Conference in 2000 was that 'no countries seriously committed to education for all will be thwarted in their achievement of this goal by a lack of resources' (UNESCO 2000a: paragraph 10). The FTI was conceived initially as a direct response to this promise. It was established in 2002, following a proposal from the World Bank made at a donor's conference in the Netherlands, as an international partnership designed to accelerate progress towards the achievement of universal primary completion by 2015. Raising additional resources to support countries with credible education plans to achieve the MDGs was the initial central intention. It was anticipated that it would become the main vehicle by which the financial gaps preventing the achievement of the education MDGs would be removed.

In that regard its subsequent progress has been disappointing. By 2006, only some 20 countries had achieved fully endorsed sector programmes within the FTI. With few exceptions, these were the smaller developing countries, having a combined total number of out-of-school children of around 16 million – only about one seventh of the global total (FTI Secretariat 2005). More significantly, even for those 20 countries, only some $453 million had been raised by FTI for disbursement between 2003 and 2007 – less than half the monies required to close their anticipated funding gaps (FTI Secretariat 2006). Thus, achieving the central objective for which FTI was established appears to have been elusive: the total aid raised by FTI represents only a small proportion of the estimated $10 billion per year in aid needed in order to reach universal primary completion in all low-income countries by 2015.

In response to this experience, the emphasis of FTI has shifted to giving strong weight to the process of building development partnerships between donors and recipients. A major intention has become to strengthen domestic capacity in education planning and analysis and to facilitate increased transfers of aid resources via the 'normal' channels, as opposed to separate parallel mechanisms. The jury is still out as to whether this approach can be successful in the absence of demonstrated fund-raising capacity. Providing successful support for national planning is crucially dependent upon a coincidence of motivation and interests of both the donor group and the national government. At least in some country cases, the lack of success with the financing facility has led to tensions between the government and FTI, owing to strong expectations that additional funding would be forthcoming, encouraged by the FTI, not in fact being met.

In addition, it is not yet clear whether the FTI instrument alone will be capable of generating additional resources through existing bilateral and multilateral channels. There is evidence that, even where donors and partner governments see it as being in their interests to produce a sector plan that subsequently gets endorsed, and has associated funding gaps articulated within it, the moral suasion available to FTI is insufficient to secure increased pledges from the donors represented in the countries concerned, so as to enable the funding gaps to be met. As argued elsewhere (Colclough and Fennell 2005), this is partly a manifestation of the classic problem of 'collective action', whereby individual donors have an incentive to free-ride on the actions of others in the group (a seminal analysis of the general case of problems of collective action is provided by Olsen 1965). Where the provision of additional resources to secure universal primary completion in partner countries can benefit all parties to the exercise, irrespective of their source, the incentives for agencies to act individually are thereby weakened. This tendency is further aggravated by the relatively weak position of field office staff compared with those working at agency headquarters. Local ability to authorise increases in aid allocations is usually very limited, and at the centre there is typically strong competition and argument about resource allocation within and between sectors and countries. Thus, existing commitments against an already stretched aid budget usually prevent the rapid allocation of additional funds to FTI or other uses at the national level. Under these circumstances, it cannot be surprising that the funding gaps approved at the national level are not quickly covered by a flexible donor response.

Conclusion

It is reasonable to conclude that both the international mechanisms for encouraging developing country governments to reform domestic policy in support of EFA and those intended to secure increased levels of financing from international agency sources for the same purposes are not yet fully fit for purpose. We have argued that UNESCO recently enhanced its ability to monitor, provide commentary on and analyse the different rates of progress towards EFA that are manifest around the world and to explain their main causes. However, although the power of analysis is itself considerable, the organisation has not yet managed to finesse the clear shifts in national and international policies that its analysis demonstrates are required. It is this aspect of UNESCO's role that particularly needs to be strengthened. Although some ways of doing so are at hand, we must also recognise that, since it is not a development finance institution, UNESCO is not naturally able to utilise mechanisms that can secure significant national policy change. Mainly because it has few resources, it does not have policy leverage in the ways that characterise the work of the international finance institutions. Accordingly, notwithstanding the expectations of Dakar, de facto leadership of the EFA process has been more strongly assumed by the World Bank and by some of the bilateral agencies such as DFID. Yet their own success in designing and operationalising new instruments with the policy and financial leverage required for securing EFA has been disappointing. Although initially hailed by some as a potential global fund for securing EFA, the FTI has worked more as an instrument for harmonising the aid dialogue than for securing additional funding. Policy leadership requires more than advocacy if it is to be effective. A much clearer process for establishing individual agency responsibility for contributing to funding gaps will be needed if the present country-based practice of trying to secure the required resources remains in place.

References

Chowdhury, S and Squire, L. (2006) Setting weights for aggregate indices: An application to the commitment to Development Index and Human Development Index. *Journal of Development Studies*, 42(5): 761-771.

Colclough, C. (2004) Towards universal primary education. In Black, R and White, H (eds). *Targeting Development – Critical Perspectives on the Millennium Development Goals*. London: Routledge, 166-183.

Colclough, C. (2005) Rights, goals and targets: How do those for education add up? *Journal of International Development*, 17: 101-111.

Colclough, C, Al-Samarrai, S, Rose, P and Tembon, M. (2003) *Achieving Schooling for All in Africa: Costs, Commitment and Gender.* Aldershot: Ashgate.

Colclough, C and Fennell, S. (2005) *The Fast Track Initiative: Towards a New strategy for Meeting the Education MDGs.* Report to DFID (mimeo), London.

Colclough, C, with Lewin, K. (1993) *Educating All the Children: Strategies for Primary Schooling in the South.* Oxford: Clarendon Press.

FTI Secretariat. (2005) Progress report prepared for the EFA-FTI Partnership Meeting, Washington, December 2005.

FTI Secretariat. (2006) January-April 2006 Newsletter, Washington.

ILO/UNCTAD. (2001) *The Minimum Income for School Attendance Initiative.* Geneva: ILO/UNCTAD Advisory Group.

Lavinas, L. (2001) *The Appeal of Minimum Income Programmes in Latin America.* Geneva: ILO.

OECD DAC. (1996) *Shaping the 21st Century: The Contribution of Development Cooperation.* Paris: OECD.

Olsen, M. (1965) *The Logic of Collective Action.* Cambridge, Mass: Harvard University Press.

Rose, P. (1995) Female education and adjustment programmes: A cross-country statistical analysis. *World Development,* 23(1): 1931-1949.

Tomasevski, K. (2003) *School fees as hindrance to universalizing primary education.* Background paper for EFA Global Monitoring Report 2003/4 (mimeo).

UN. (2001) Resolution A/56/326, 6 September 2001, United Nations General Assembly, New York.

UNDP. (2004) *Human Development Report 2004: Cultural Liberty in Today's Diverse World.* New York: Oxford University Press.

UNESCO. (2000a) *The Dakar Framework for Action. Education for All: Meeting our Collective Commitments.* Paris: UNESCO.

UNESCO. (2000b) *World Education Forum – Final Report.* Paris: UNESCO.

UNESCO. (2003) *EFA Global Monitoring Report 2003/4: Gender and Education for All -The Leap to Equality.* Paris: UNESCO.

UNESCO. (2005) *EFA Global Monitoring Report 2006: Education for All - Literacy for Life.* Paris: UNESCO.

UNESCO. (2006) *EFA Global Monitoring Report 2007: Strong Foundations – Early Childhood Care and Education.* Paris: UNESCO.

UN Millennium Project. (2005) *Taking Action: Achieving Gender Equality and Empowering Women.* London: Earthscan.

Universalia. (2006) *Formative Review of the Education for All Global*

Monitoring Report. Volume II, Narrative Report. Paris: UNESCO.
Unterhalter, E. (2005) Fragmented frameworks? Researching women, gender, education and development. In Aikman, S and Unterhalter, E
(eds). *Beyond Access: Transforming Policy and Practice for Gender
Equality in Education.* Oxford: Oxfam, 15-35.

---

[1] In addition to three earlier human rights treaties, these include the Convention
on the Elimination of all Forms of Discrimination against Women and the Convention on the Rights of the Child, which came into force in 1981 and 1990
respectively. Both of these include specific requirements to guarantee non-
discriminatory rights of access to and provision of education.

[2] For more discussion of these parallel legal and political processes, and of the
specific undertakings made by signatories to the agreements, see Colclough
2005. A detailed description of the rights to education and to gender equality
specified by international treaties and declarations is given in UNESCO 2003:
Appendix 1.

[3] This was also evident in the selection of task forces set up, under the Millennium Project, to report on progress towards the goals during 2005. There were
ten of these, but Task Force 3 was asked to report on both the education and the
gender goals (Goals 2 and 3). Task Force members soon found it necessary to
have two reports – one on education and one on gender equality – with education being recognized as fundamental for the latter, yet comprising only one of
the gender report's seven strategic priorities for policy change (UN Millennium
Project 2005: 28-29).

[4] An earlier paper (Colclough 2004) identified the main cost and national expenditure constraints to achieving UPE, concluding that the 2015 targets are
achievable, subject to national governments introducing new efficiency measures, increasing educational expenditures and promoting a range of quality and
demand-side reforms. The aid requirements were also specified. Hence, the
present discussion of whether the goals can be achieved is restricted to a discussion of the nature and feasibility of the reform process itself within the
time-scale required, and particularly to the role of the international community
in this process.

[5] The experience of targeted income supplementation schemes such as Progresa
in Mexico and Bolsa Escola in Brazil demonstrates the potential effectiveness
of conditional subsidies as a means of reducing the opportunity costs of school
attendance and of increasing school enrolments (ILO/UNCTAD 2001; Lavinas
2001). The sustainablility of such schemes is often a key constraint, but with

careful targeting the impact on unit costs can be surprisingly small. Examples for six African countries are shown in Colclough et al 2003: Table 6.3.

[6] The indicators for each of the goals are: net enrolment ratio in primary education as an indicator of progress towards UPE; literacy rate of those aged 15 years and over, as an indicator of adult literacy; survival rate to grade 5 as an indicator of the quality of education; simple average of gender parity indices for primary and secondary education and for adult literates, as an indicator of the gender goal. The other two 'Dakar' goals – for the enhancement of early childhood education and of life-skills programmes – do not yet have indicators that are conducive to quantitative measurement on an international basis.

[7] See, for example, UNDP 2004: 258-264, where the methods and associated technical problems of constructing the Human Development Index, and the other indices used by the Human Development Report, are outlined. A recent assessment has concluded that the unitary weights accorded to the items in the HDI roughly accord with professional opinion as to their relative importance (Chowdhury and Squire 2006).

[8] This is not to imply disingenuousness on the part of either government or agency representatives. Often, policies had indeed changed, and the data did reveal some improvement the following year. The differences were, however, rarely sufficient to change national or agency rankings in very significant ways.

Why some Education for All and Millennium Development Goals will not be met: Difficulties with goals and targets

Keith LEWIN

This article argues that for a significant number of sub-Saharan African (SSA) countries, the Education for All (EFA) goals and the Millennium Development Goals (MDGs) referring to education are unlikely to be achieved by 2015 but that with substantial external assistance countries at risk should make better progress. It argues that this will be possible only if (1) current status and starting points are clearly recognised, (2) links are made between the EFA and MDG goals, national development strategies on poverty reduction and theoretical considerations on the role of education in development, (3) access and equity issues are re-conceptualised to reflect aspirations and specific patterns of participation, and (4) targets and indicative benchmarks adapted to context and starting points are adopted that nurture relationships between target-setters and getters and reconcile ambitions with sustainable financial demands across the education sector.

Status report

The Global Monitoring Report (UNESCO, 2004) indicates that 47 countries worldwide had universal primary education by 2002. It estimates a further 20 may succeed by 2015, and 20 are considered at risk of not achieving the goal. A further 47 have little chance of achieving the goal or are judged very unlikely to succeed. About half of these are in sub-Saharan Africa (SSA).

Forty-nine countries had achieved gender equity at primary and secondary levels by 2002 and 14 were considered likely to do so by 2015. Seventy-nine were considered at risk of not achieving parity in enrolments by 2015, 43 of which are likely to fail because of inequity at secondary level and 24 at primary and secondary level. The majority of those likely to fail only at secondary level have more girls than boys enrolled; in contrast the majority of those likely to fail at both levels have more boys than girls enrolled. Most of these are in SSA.

Recent estimates suggest there are about 108 million primary school age children in SSA, about 91 million of whom are enrolled. At secondary level there are 92 million children and about 25 million enrolled. This means that at least 17 million children of primary school age and 67 million of secondary school age are out of school. In reality the numbers are much greater, since enrolment figures include large numbers of over-age pupils and repeaters. Enrolment estimates also fail to capture those who may be registered but not attending. Though reliable estimates of those not attending school across SSA are not available, it is reasonable to conclude that more than 25 million in the primary age group and 75 million of secondary age are excluded through not being enrolled or through being nominally enrolled but not attending.

What can we conclude? In the majority of SSA countries there are not yet enough school places to enrol all school age children at primary level, and many more are excluded from lower secondary schooling than primary. Secondary enrolments in lower-income SSA countries are very low, though lower secondary is increasingly seen as part of basic education and EFA (Lewin 2006b). Universal access to primary is becoming a problem for the 'last 20%', who are likely to be from the poorest sections of the population. The numbers excluded at secondary level are much greater than at primary level, and there is a predominance of children from households with high levels of income at secondary schools. Expanding fee-paying secondary schooling has equity implications that may result in greater than current differentiation and polarisation of access.

EFA goals and MDG targets
The EFA goals (UNESCO 2000) have set an agenda for educational development in SSA that has been widely influential in shaping national plans and external assistance. The EFA goals are as follows:

1.   Expanding and improving comprehensive early childhood care and education, especially for the most vulnerable and disadvan-

taged children

2. Ensuring that by 2015 all children, particularly girls, children in difficult circumstances and those belonging to ethnic minorities, have access to complete free and compulsory primary education of good quality

3. Ensuring that the learning needs of all young people and adults are met through equitable access to appropriate learning and life skills programmes

4. Achieving a 50% improvement in levels of adult literacy by 2015, especially for women, and equitable access to basic and continuing education for all adults

5. Eliminating gender disparities in primary and secondary education by 2005, and achieving gender equality in education by 2015, with a focus on ensuring girls' full and equal access to and achievement in basic education of good quality

6. Improving all aspects of the quality of education and ensuring excellence so that recognized and measurable learning outcomes are achieved by all, especially in literacy, numeracy and essential life skills

Three of these goals (2,4,5) can readily be translated into quantitative targets, although each retains qualitative dimensions, and three others (1,3,6) require judgements and can to some extent be proxied by data on access and learning outcomes. The EFA goals have been reinforced by the adoption of the MDGs (United Nations 2000), two of which (MDG2 – Achieve universal primary education by 2015, and MDG3 – Promote gender equality and empower women through eliminating gender disparity in enrolment at primary and secondary level by 2005) overlap directly with the EFA goals. Much could be said about problems with the specification of these laudable goals and their uneven translation into policy and practice. Six points suffice.

First, predictably, goals with an apparently clear quantitative definition have been given far more prominence than those which require judgement and contextualisation. Thus achieving enrolment rate targets – first of 100% primary enrolment, then 100% net enrolment rates (NERs) and now 100% completion to the end of primary, and parity in enrolments of girls and boys at primary and more recently secondary levels – have overshadowed attempts to address other EFA goals.

Second, some of these universal goals have a long history. International efforts to achieve universal primary education (UPE) date back to the UNESCO conferences of the 1960s, and more recently to the UPE targets for 2000 set at the 1990 Jomtien conference. Where time-bound targets have not been met in the past, they have been rolled forward, often without considered analysis of the reasons for failure. The gender parity goal for 2005 was missed and has similarly been rolled forward to 2015.

Third, although the goals appear to be independent of each other, in practice they interact and imply other goals that would need to be met if the primary goal is to be attained. Thus UPE cannot be achieved without an adequate supply of teachers drawn from increased numbers of secondary school graduates; universal primary completion is unlikely unless transition rates into secondary schooling are high enough to maintain motivation to complete primary; universal access to primary necessarily implies gender parity in enrolments; the investment required to substantially expand access to early childhood care and education competes with the resource demands of universal primary; improving adult literacy over 10 to 15 years may be most rapidly achieved by ensuring that all those who attend school leave literate.

Fourth, starting points are very different in different systems and the distance to be travelled varies widely. In some cases the goals will not be challenging because they have already been achieved; in others they will be unattainable and lack plausibility.

Fifth, the goals as specified mix rights-based approaches to service delivery with aspirations to achieve developmentally desirable outcomes. These may conflict. Thus including the last 20% in primary schooling may alleviate poverty less than investing in more equitable access to secondary schooling; meeting the special educational needs of some sub-populations may deny access to others.

Sixth, operational goals need to be converted to targets. If target-setters are not target-getters there is a risk that target ownership will be diffuse, accountability for target achievement unclear and methods of assessing success ambiguous. Amongst the problems that can arise are difficulties in translating macro targets – e.g. 100% enrolment of primary age children – into meaningful activities at lower administrative levels (who is responsible for ensuring all children attend?), problems of motivation and reward (what is the consequence of meeting or failing to meet targets institutionally and individually?) and issues concerned with assessing goal achievement (which definition of completion rates is appropriate, and how easy or difficult is it to assess net enrolment rates?).

Underlying these and other problems are three sets of issues.

The first is the lack of articulation of the EFA goals and MDGs with development theory linking investment in education with developmentally desirable outcomes and specific national contexts.

The second is that achieving the set goals requires analytic purchase on the nature of the problems that have prevented them from being achieved in the past and, with changing circumstances, may prevent them from being achieved in the future. Re-conceptualising the challenges presented by the goals in a contextually grounded way is a prerequisite for evidence-based policy that might just succeed where past attempts have failed.

The third is to revisit the issues that surround the EFA goals and MDGs and the indicative targets and benchmarks they generate. This is needed to develop sustainable implementation plans that can be financed with an appropriate mix of domestic revenue and external assistance. The next sections discuss these issues.

Theoretical perspectives on development, EFA and the MDGs

The discourse surrounding EFA and the MDGs is not grounded in any explicit single set of propositions about the role of education in development and the extent to which educational access and achievement are of themselves part of development. This is perhaps not unexpected given the nature of the process through which the EFA goals were generated and the geo-political dimensions of gaining consensus for the MDGs. However, without propositional frameworks that link educational investment and desired developmental outcomes, albeit with different contextual nuances, there are obvious risks that even if EFA goals are achieved, development more broadly defined may not take place.

Arguably the events that led to the Jomtien conference were underpinned by a kind of 'Washington consensus' that development could be accelerated through investment in human capital, that a new thrust to universalise primary education was needed because social rates of return at this level were generally very positive, that the developmental benefits of schooling were substantial (greater agricultural productivity, lower infant mortality and morbidity, etc.) and that economic growth (and just possibly improved income distribution, political stability and better governance) would follow from raising the average educational level of the poor. The result was a shift from a previous emphasis on higher-level skills development (technical and vocational education, higher education investment) to a growing prioritisation of basic education that could be externally supported as a vector for development. Though this did not meet with initial enthusiasm on the part of at least some SSA governments, gradually it became a dominant orthodoxy.

Developments were also shaped by post-colonial political events. Most obviously, African socialist approaches to development lost ground, partly as a result of their own failures to generate development and partly as a result of the collapse of sponsors amongst the socialist states of Eastern Europe and market-oriented transformations in China. Neo-liberalism began to hold sway with strong messages about marketisation of service delivery, smaller state bureaucracies and more integration into the world economy.

Most recently, since the Dakar World Education Forum (2000), rights-based approaches have gained prominence in the international debates, stressing that equitable access to reasonable quality education is denied to large proportions of the population of many developing countries, that this is unacceptable and that both governments and development partners have obligations to deliver on commitments they have made. Debt relief tied to educational investment has become a reality, and, through a variety of mechanisms including the Fast Track Initiative, development partners have pledged to support countries that produce viable educational development plans. The G8 has made clear its intentions to transform the volumes and modalities of external assistance.

Meanwhile, globalisation has become a new reality for most of SSA, with impacts on rights-based approaches to education and development, for instance through the activities of international NGOs, and on educational practice and process in areas such as convergence in curricula and examining systems, advocacy of child-centred pedagogies, cross-national monitoring of achievement and introduction of capitation funding systems. Information on every aspect of educational practice and process is more widely available than in earlier periods and this will further increase with the spread of information technology. External assistance programmes have become more homogeneous with the development of sector-wide approaches and general budget support reflecting the desire to replace ad hoc project support with sector-wide plans supported by several development partners. In developing educational plans that qualify for external assistance, various benchmarks and indicative frameworks now exist that generate convergence, at least at national level. These tend to be normative more often than not, based on best-practice, selective comparisons with 'successful countries' and convenient rules of thumb. However, they are also formative in that they compress complex system realities into homogenising policy and practice.

The theoretical underpinning of EFA and the MDGs is beyond the scope of this article. However, reflection in this area provokes some key dilemmas that need addressing if the goals and targets set are to endure and be translated into the kind of poverty reduction, equity and growth assumed to be at the core of development.

First, though it is fairly obvious that increased productivity, which generates wealth, is associated with higher levels of knowledge and skill, how this equation operates in many SSA economies remains largely unknown. What kind of knowledge and skills are appropriate, one may ask, which leads to questions of curriculum, teaching and learning, and how do these relate to productivity, whether in agriculture, the informal sector, the modern sector or elsewhere?

Second, though it is easy to demonstrate in every SSA country that the more educated have higher incomes, and that *ipso facto* educational access is poverty alleviating, how this is changing with expanded access is unclear. Most obviously the high rates of return associated with primary schooling are likely to be falling as labour markets saturate with primary school graduates. There is some evidence of concave rates of return developing with little additional benefit to those who continue to attend for additional years until they reach a threshold of scarcity, which may now be upper secondary or higher education.

Third, achieving EFA and the MDGs is increasingly a problem in terms of reaching the last 20%. One orthodoxy is that there may be a threshold of acquired basic education (and for that matter literacy) below which sustained development is unlikely. However, there may also be an upper threshold above which investment in extending access to basic education is essentially consumption to increase social welfare rather than poverty alleviation. Almost certainly the rate of return on the margin will be low, since in accessing difficult to reach groups with special needs the costs of provision are likely to be above-average. Subsequent economic benefits are likely to be below-average.

Fourth, thresholds may also apply to the pursuit of gender equity in schooling. Where differences in enrolments between boys and girls are large (greater than 5%?), then the transaction costs of special intervention programmes may be justified if demonstrably effective. At some threshold (partly determined by overall enrolment rates) it may be more cost-effective to focus resources on increasing overall enrolment whilst maintaining gender equitable policy and practice.

Fifth, equity of educational access in SSA is most strongly determined by household income (Lewin 2006c). The effects on access generally decrease in the early primary grades, but usually increase as drop-out differentially affects the poor. Access to secondary schooling is strongly related to household income. Differences between rural and urban access can be striking, especially where most secondary provision is urban or peri-urban. Gender differences in SSA are almost always greater at secondary level than at primary. There are developmental questions: whether equity is conceived of at the individual or household level (bearing in mind also average family size) and whether it is more important to address inequity at primary level, which affects more students, or at secondary level, where inequity is much greater.

Sixth, decentralisation is widely promoted as a mechanism that should enhance progress towards the EFA goals and the MDGs. But this is not self-evidently the case. There are several issues. These include clarity about what is to be decentralised – school governance is very different from curriculum development, text book production or section examinations.

Decentralised school financing may be attractive if capacity exists to manage funds, accountability and audit are effective and formula funding or some other mechanism can generate consistent and reliable disbursement. It may also fail where bottlenecks exist in disbursement, checks and balances are ineffective and administrative capacity is weak.

Local authorities may or may not share national priorities and the micro politics of local power structures may be exclusive rather than inclusive. Seventh, the role of the private sector in achieving EFA and the MDGs remains a constant source of debate, as it does with other forms of public service delivery. It is clear that experience from other sectors, such as water and health, cannot be directly applied to educational service provision (Lewin 2006a, Lewin and Sayed 2005). Once the principle of universal free primary schooling is accepted, it is clear that private providers should only recruit those able to pay on an elective basis. No such clarity exists above primary level in much of SSA. Most secondary schooling is fee-paying, and often, even in public systems, the bulk of the costs are privately supported from fees and other contributions. However, various analyses demonstrate that full-cost non-state schooling in low enrolment SSA is unlikely to be affordable to those outside the top 20% of household incomes. This limits the extent to which expanded access will be provided by unsubsidised non-state providers.

Eighth, several SSA countries, such as Nigeria, Tanzania, Uganda and Zambia, have nearly achieved universal primary education in the past but have been unable to sustain it. The more obvious causes – conflict and civil unrest, economic mismanagement and macroeconomic failure, the impact of HIV and AIDS, lack of administrative capacity – have to be analysed with the less obvious, such as lack of sustained political will, ineffective regional policies, discrimination against particular social groups, internal and cross-border migration, and poor professional practice.

Reconceptualising access in the context of EFA and the MDGs

The most prominent target for EFA and the education MDGs relates to universalising access to primary schooling (or more generally now basic education through to grade 9). This article argues that reconceptualisation is needed if this is to be achieved in SSA, building on work undertaken by the Consortium for Research on Educational Access, Transitions and Equity (CREATE – www.create-rpc.org).

Access issues

The central problem EFA and the MDGs address is how to increase meaningful access for girls and boys between the ages of five and 15.

The numbers are large. Even where gross primary enrolment rates exceed 100%, national data indicate that attendance may be below 70%, completion rates may fall below 50%, and fewer than 20% may attend lower secondary. Achievement data often show a minority acquiring basic learning skills by grade 5. The EFA Global Monitoring Reports (UNESCO 2002-2005) indicate the scale of the challenge, and its changing urban and rural characteristics.

Initial enrolment and progression are a result of the interaction of both supply *and* demand. Many EFA programmes present access as a supply-side issue that can be resolved if enough school places are provided. This was always insufficient to achieve schooling for all (Colclough with Lewin, 1993). The supply of school places remains important for those initially excluded and for those learning under conditions that compromise successful achievement. Critical supply-side issues include school location, teacher deployment and training, availability of learning materials, and safety, especially for girls (see e.g. Dunne and Leach 2004; Lewin and Stuart, 2003; Colclough et al. 2003). However, since the Jomtien conference, expanded enrolments have not always been accompanied by falling repetition and drop-out. For instance, in Malawi the number of primary school completers has remained static over ten years despite a 60% overall increase in enrolments. Demand may soften as gross enrolment rates (GERs) rise.

Patterns of demand shape entry, progression, completion and transition to lower secondary, and are often gendered. Rapidly expanding enrolments have been associated with changing perceptions of the relevance and effectiveness of schooling and of the benefits of participation (Lewin and Caillods 2001). The problems of capturing and retaining the last 20%, and increasing promotion, completion and transition, are inextricably linked to decisions to participate. These are partly related to the direct costs of schooling but are also dependent on 'family strategies' (Laugharn 2001) and many other factors. How demand has been changing, and how supply interacts with demand, are central concerns (Mukudi 2004; Boyle et al. 2002; Rose and Al-Samarrai 2001; Canagarajah and Nielsen 1999; Ravallion and Wodon 1999).

Exclusion from basic education is a process culminating in an event with many causes. A new research programme, CREATE, uses the term 'zones of vulnerability' to describe the various spaces where children are included, excluded or at risk. Initial access has little meaning unless it results in (1) regular attendance, (2) progression, (3) meaningful learning and (4) appropriate access to post-primary education. Children falling into these zones of vulnerability are the subject of our research, especially disadvantaged groups, such as girls, HIV/AIDS orphans, displaced people and ethnic minorities. Figure 3.1 presents a cross-sectional model of access. It illustrates how enrolments decline through the primary grades and how those attending irregularly and achieving poorly fall into 'at risk' zones. In this hypothetical model half of the primary completers are selected into lower secondary school. where attrition continues (Lewin 2007).

Figure 3.1: Access and zones of exclusion from primary and secondary schooling

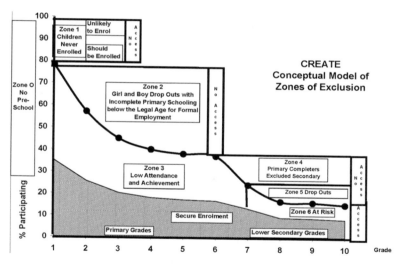

Zone 1 contains those denied any access. Expansion of conventional schooling can enrol a proportion of these children, but is unlikely to embrace all by 2015. More research is needed on the circumstances that surround those without access to orthodox schooling, e.g. nomadic groups (Aikman and el Haj 2005), those in low population density areas (Little 2006) and those in extreme poverty (Kabeer et al. 2003), to establish how their basic education needs might best be met. This additional research could identify whether different modes of service delivery offer promise (Chowdury et al. 2003) and whether opportunities to join mainstream schooling will be sufficient to extend access to all. It is likely that the best solution for most of those currently excluded from grade 1 is extending the reach of the existing formal system. Analysis is needed of the gaps in provision (both rural and urban) and of feasible, pro-poor and affordable strategies. These should recognise the growing attention being given to pre-school.

Zone 2 includes the great majority of children who are excluded *after* initial entry. Typically, drop-out is greatest in the early grades, with a substantial subsequent push-out at the transition to secondary school. Precursors to drop-out include repetition, low achievement, previous temporary withdrawals, low attendance, late enrolment, poor teaching, degraded facilities, very large classes, household poverty, child labour and poor health and nutrition (Boyle et al. 2002; Canagarajah and Nielsen 1999; Fentiman, Hall and Bundy 1999; Nokes et al. 1998). Those dropping out usually become permanently excluded with no pathway back to re-enter. The zone includes disproportionate numbers of girls, HIV/AIDS orphans and others in vulnerable circumstances (Pridmore et al. 2005). It may be influenced by child labour practices (Ravallion and Wodon 1999).

Zone 3 includes those in school but at risk of dropping out. These children might be low-attenders, repeaters and low-achievers. Children who remain formally enrolled in school may be silently excluded if their attendance is sporadic, if their achievement is so low that they cannot follow the curriculum or if they are discriminated against for socio-cultural reasons. Nutritional deficiencies and sickness can compound these problems. Too little is known of how the range of influential factors is changing as EFA evolves, how they result in decisions to enrol and attend at different grade/age levels, and how they impact on different key disadvantaged groups.

Zone 4 contains those excluded from lower secondary school as a result of failing to be selected, being unable to afford the costs or dropping out before successful completion of primary. This exclusion is important for EFA, since transition rates into secondary affect demand for primary schooling, primary teacher supply depends on secondary graduates, and gender equity at the secondary level is an MDG. Access to secondary schooling promotes the social mobility needed to give poor households more access to higher-income employment.

Zone 5 includes those children who have entered lower secondary school but who fail to progress to the end of the cycle. In most countries lower secondary is now considered part of basic education. Many who fail to complete the cycle are likely to be below the legal working age if they are in the appropriate grade for their age. The reasons for drop-out include poor performance, affordability and loss of interest. Demand to remain in school may weaken as a result of high opportunity costs where work is available.

Zone 6 contains lower secondary children at risk of drop-out. As with Zone 3, some will be silently excluded though enrolled and at risk as a result of poor attendance and low achievement. Costs and affordability are also likely to be significant.

Zone 0 refers to pre-school participation. This is very poorly detailed, though it is clear that in low enrolment countries large majorities experience little or no access to organised pre-school, and those that do are often enrolled in high-cost private facilities. This almost certainly disadvantages this population in relation to those that do attend pre-school and achieve a head start in basic learning. Several countries are developing policies to extend the reach of pre-schooling and provide public finance to support its development (e.g. Ghana and South Africa).

Political, social, cultural and institutional conditions exist alongside economic realities. Together they frame the interaction of educational supply and demand at the individual, household, community and system level within each of the seven zones. These factors are widely overlooked in relation to EFA policy and planning. They include, *inter alia,* livelihood conditions (e.g. Buchman and Brakewood 2000), political climates (Little 1999), institutional arrangements (e.g. Birdsall et al. 2005), cultural and religious affiliations (Daun 2000) and gender issues (Colclough et al 2003). Almost every EFA/MDG report calls for enhanced political leadership and commitment to the goals of EFA/MDG. However, we know little about the conditions under which politicians see it as in their interests to support EFA and go beyond the rhetoric of expanding basic education to act to improve access for the poor and disadvantaged.

It is possible to profile participation in SSA in terms of different patterns of access. These generate starting points for progress towards EFA and the education MDGs. SSA countries fall into five broad groups in terms of existing patterns of access. There are those with –

1. high participation in primary and secondary, with low rates of repetition and drop-out;
2. very high initial enrolment rates in primary but high drop-out and repetition with low completion rates, and falling transition rates into secondary and low participation at secondary;
3. high primary entry rates and mid-levels of repetition, drop-out and completion, with mid-range secondary participation;
4. primary entry rates below universal levels, and low primary and secondary enrolment rates; and
5. very low primary entry rates and very low participation at primary and secondary school.

These patterns are illustrated in Figure 3.2, showing how participation falls by grade for each group of countries. The patterns vary greatly and create different starting points for investment. Where the participation index (the number enrolled/the number in the age group for the grade) is around 100% through to grade 9, then most are already enrolled through primary and into lower secondary (type 1). In type 2 initial entry is much greater than the number of children of grade 1 age. However, participation rapidly falls off so that by grade 6 enrolments are only about 20% of the age group. Type 3 countries have fewer over-age pupils in grade 1 and manage to retain more of them through to grade 9 than is the case for type 2. Type 4 and 5 systems fail to enrol many children in grade 1 and have low and very low participation rates at grade 9. Countries with patterns 4 and 5 may come to resemble pattern 2 if UPE programmes are introduced rapidly. However, ideally future expansion will not create the exaggerated patterns of Type 2 whereby massive over-enrolment in grade 1 is accompanied by high drop-out and little improvement in secondary participation rates. If it does, then the difficulties associated with falling transition rates into secondary will be exacerbated.

Figure 3.2: Generic chart of enrolment patterns

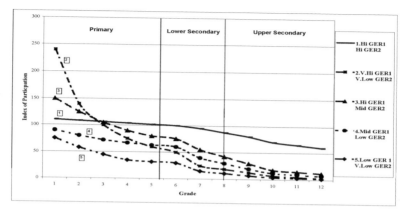

Source: Lewin 2006c

These patterns suggest different policy priorities for countries in different groups. Some indication of possible options is provided in Figure 3.3.

In summary, it is necessary to reconceptualise access and equity issues to understand –

- the different participation patterns that shape policies aimed at universalising access; this includes consideration of the inter-actions between primary and secondary expansion, especially as they relate to teacher supply and transition rates;
- the characteristics of those in the different zones of exclusion, particularly the fact that the majority who are not enrolled have attended, but dropped out;
- the significance for EFA of attendance and 'silent exclusion';
- the balance between supply-side and demand-side constraints;
- the political economy of EFA;
- the extent of exclusion related to household income;
- the degree to which gendered exclusion is related to structural factors, the extent of participation at different grade levels, and differential entry ages and rates of drop-out;
- the need to link conceptualisations to sustainable financial frameworks for resource allocation.

Targets and indicative benchmarks – panacea or problem?

Some of the issues surrounding targets set for EFA and the MDGs have been discussed above. Their use has generated various indicative frameworks and benchmarks that are in general use in relation to external assistance. The reasons are easily understandable. Clarity is needed regarding objectives, external assistance needs to be justified against measurable outcomes and recipients of assistance need to be specific about what they are agreeing to achieve with the support they receive.

Inevitably the idea is simpler than its execution. Table 3.1 lists a small number of the most common currently used benchmarks: in some planning processes the number exceeds 50 indicators.

Several issues arise that are discussed further in Lewin (2005).

First, these benchmarks do not constitute a single list. Different development partners stress different elements and the list of common targets has changed over the last ten years. Thus there may be an element of 'pick and mix' when it comes to applying targets to different systems. This is helpful if it reflects varying contexts; it may be confusing if the basis for choice is arbitrary. Identifying desirable pupil: teacher ratios, class size, teachers' salaries as a percentage of GDP, the proportion of private sector provision and other factors acquire very different meanings in different systems, since starting points are so different and prospects for the achievement of goals so varied.

Second, the types of benchmark and their derivation varies. Sometimes they are absolute outcomes, as with 100% enrolled in primary. In other cases they reflect what is judged to be best practice, as in a 40:1 pupil/teacher ratio at primary level. In yet other cases they may be based on abstract analysis of, for example, finance and unit costs leading to advocacy of particular target levels, such as primary teachers' salaries at 3,5 times GDP per capita. Other possibilities include best case comparison, such as level of achievement in cross-country comparisons, proportional progress (halving the illiteracy rate) and statistical redistribution (equity gains reflected in the distribution of participation by household income). Which types of targets are identified and on what basis clearly has implications for the extent to which they may be understood, accepted and acted on. It may also shape which groups' interests may be threatened, and which supported, when decisions are made on resource allocation.

Figure 3.3: Typology of challenges for the expansion of primary and secondary schooling in SSA

	Description	Countries	Prognosis
1	High GER1, high GER2L and GER2U, low attrition	Seychelles, South Africa, Botswana, Mauritius, Namibia, Zimbabwe, Swaziland	High participation rates at all levels and low population growth. Mostly higher income. Secondary expansion needed is modest and likely to be well within domestic resources.
2	Very high GER1, very low GER2L and GER2U, high attrition	Uganda, Rwanda, Malawi, Madagascar, Mozambique, Tanzania	High GER1, but high attrition through primary grades. Transition rates likely to fall as large numbers of primary entrants flow through to the last grade of primary. Very high rates of secondary expansion needed to maintain transition rates. Financing of secondary expansion problematic, even with reforms. More investment in primary quality, reduced repetition and higher completion needed.
3	High GER1, mid-range GER2L and GER2U, mid-range attrition	Togo, Lesotho, São Tomé and Príncipe, Nigeria, Benin, Cameroon	High GER 1 with mid-range attrition through primary. Difficult to maintain transition rates if primary completion rates increase. Secondary expansion needed to enrol more than 50% through lower secondary. Financing of secondary expansion feasible, but requires reforms.
4	Mid-range GER1, low GER2L and GER2U, mid-range attrition	Gambia, Zambia, Kenya, Comoros, Congo, Ghana, Cote d'Ivoire	GER1 below 100 with substantial numbers not enrolling or completing primary. Mid-range attrition reflects low initial enrolment, high repetition and drop-out. Transition rates mid-range but participation in secondary low. Substantial expansion needed to reach 50% in lower secondary. Financing of secondary expansion challenging, and in competition with need for more investment to increase GER1. Strategic focus needed.
5	Low GER1, very low GER2L and GER2U, mid-range attrition	Guinea, Tanzania, Eritrea, Ethiopia, Senegal, Mali, Guinea-Bissau, Burundi, Chad, Burkina Faso, Niger	Low GER 1 with most not completing primary. Mid-range attrition reflects low entry rates, high repetition and drop-out. Transition rates mid-range but participation in secondary very low. Massive expansion needed to reach 50% GER in lower secondary. Priority likely to be to finance increased primary participation in advance of modest rates of strategically focused expansion at secondary.

Table 3.1: Indicative benchmarks from various sources

Benchmark	Indicative indicator at primary level	Comment
Service delivery		
Average annual teacher's salary (as multiple of GDP per capita)	3,5	Derived from an average of higher-enrolment countries
Unit cost per pupil as a % of GDP per capita	15%	Level necessary to afford universal enrolment
Pupil:teacher ratio	40:1	Based on pedagogic assumptions and affordability
Spending on inputs other than teachers (as a % of recurrent expenditure at the same level)	33%	Normative estimate
Average repetition rate	10% or less	Desirable norm
Intake rate girls	100%	MDG/EFA commitment
Intake rate boys	100%	MDG/EFA commitment
Completion rate girls	100%	MDG/EFA commitment
Completion rate boys	100%	MDG/EFA commitment
Survival rate to grade 5	100%	
Primary/lower secondary transition rate	No fixed target	Assumed to rise
Gross enrolment rate %	100+%	MDG/EFA commitment
Net enrolment rate %	100%	MDG/EFA commitment
Gender parity index	1	MDG/EFA commitment
Annual instructional hours	850-1 000	Cross-national comparisons
Achievement levels in national assessments	No fixed target	Assumed to increase
Achievement levels in international monitoring assessments	No fixed target	Assumed to increase
System expansion		
Construction of a classroom (unit cost)	$6 500-12 600	Based on good-practice average values in different regions
New school construction costs per classroom as a multiple of normal classroom costs	4 or less	Normative expectation
System financing		
Government revenues as % of GDP	14/16/18	Staggered targets based on levels of per capita GDP
Education budget as % of government budget	20	Minimum necessary to sustain NER 100%
Education recurrent spending as % of government revenues	20	Assuming domestic financing covers costs
Primary education recurrent spending as % of total recurrent spending	42/64	For different primary cycle lengths from 5 to 8 years
Private enrolments as % of total	10% or less	Normative expectation
Development expenditure as a % of total education expenditure	No fixed target	Depends on demand for new classrooms, schools, equipment and learning materials

Sources:
http://www.fasttrackinitiative.org/education/efafti/documents/FrameworkNOV04.pdf,
Bruns, Mingat and Raktomalala (2003), and author estimates from planning documents

Third, there are often alternative ways of measuring performance, such as 100% completion of primary schooling within the primary school age range, completion for children of any age born after a certain date, completion achieved through post-primary accreditation of those who drop out, completion defined by passing a primary school leaving certificate that has less than 100% pass, etc. The method applied clearly has implications for apparent success.

Fourth, there may be incentives to choose the most achievable definitions of standards and manipulate data to show they have been achieved. Government bureaucracies in some countries with centrally planned economies were well known for producing statistical returns claiming to meet production quotas that were artefacts of the reporting systems. If flows of external assistance depend on meeting targets, they may well appear to be met when they are not. Paradoxically, incentives may penalise the successful and reward the laggards. If the price of success is the withdrawal of subsidy and additional support to achieve the target, it may be more attractive to fall short. If the price of success is another more demanding target, the same is true. Falling short of the target, especially if the causes are lost in a fog of confused accountability, may be more attractive than success.

Fifth, if target-setters are far removed from the target-getters who have responsibility for their achievement, disjunctions may occur that lead to low levels of credibility, commitment and accountability. If chains of accountability are diffuse and spread across many organisations and organisational levels, they are unlikely to invite effective ownership. If target-setters have not had experience of target-getting, they may set unrealistic targets that lack credibility. Setting targets for levels of contribution to EFA by non-government providers is also problematic – private providers have no obvious incentive to respond to national targets.

Sixth, targets adopted by developing country governments may or may not coincide with public service agreements that development partners have with their sponsors, whether multi- or bilateral development agencies answerable to national governments or national or international NGOs with boards of directors. The scope for confusion is substantial, with many different stakeholders responsible in different ways for the achievement of targets.

Finally, targets often carry consequences for other necessary developments. More precisely, often not all desirable targets can be achieved simultaneously and there are likely to be trade-offs. Thus targets generated from wish lists are unlikely to be cumulatively feasible, and prioritisation is necessary. Interactions between targets can be very direct, as when setting targets for secondary enrolment rates implies minimum primary/secondary transition rates and primary completion rates. They may also be less direct: gender balance at secondary level may be unlikely, for instance, without high levels of primary enrolment.

Some targets interact in a zero sum way. Financially, greater public investment in primary may have to be balanced by changed levels of subsidy at other levels. This is zero sum if the education budget is determined by the level of domestic resources available, since these are relatively fixed in the short term. Decisions have to be made whether to privilege the enrolment (or completion) of every primary school child over investment at higher levels. Financial sustainability is one necessary determinant of choice, but this has to be coupled with aspects of general development strategy (where is growth to come from and what role should educational investment play?) and political reality (universities for an elite may be more politically visible than primary schooling for the rural poor).

The last point can be illustrated from recent projections of the costs of achieving EFA/MDG enrolment targets (Lewin 2006c). A data set of SSA countries with GNP/capita less than $1 500 was used to generate estimates of the costs of reaching target enrolment levels. Table 3.2 shows the results. Scenario 0 uses average levels for enrolment rates and unit costs for SSA for 2002 and allocates 20% to higher education and other expenditure. Scenario 1 simulates achieving GER1 = 110%, GER2L = 60% and GER2U = 30% and scenario 2 GER1 = 110%, GER2L = 100% and GER2U = 50%, using existing average unit costs (primary 12%, lower secondary 30% and upper secondary 60% of GNP per capita). For scenarios 3 and 4 the model is re-run using lower unit costs (primary 12%, lower secondary 20% and upper secondary 40% of GNP per capita) and lower allocations to higher education and other costs (15%).

The results show that using average SSA values of the parameters for 2002, about 2% of GNP and 50% of the education budget are required

Table 3.2: Costs of achieving different enrolment targets at different unit costs

	%GNP needed	% allocated by level
GER1 = 85, GER2L = 30, GER2U = 15		Scenario 0
Primary	1,97%	50,1%
Lower Secondary	0,77%	19,6%
Upper Secondary	0,40%	10,3%
Other incl HE	0,79%	20,0%
Total	3,93%	100,0%
GER1 = 110, GER2L = 60, GER2U = 30		Scenario 1
Primary	2,30%	36,5%
Lower Secondary	1,50%	23,8%
Upper Secondary	1,20%	19,0%
Other incl HE	1,30%	20,6%
Total	6,30%	100,0%
GER1 = 110, GER2L = 100, GER2U = 50		Scenario 2
Primary	2,30%	26,7%
Lower Secondary	2,60%	30,2%
Upper Secondary	2,00%	23,3%
Other incl HE	1,70%	19,8%
Total	8,60%	100,0%
Baseline Enrolment Targets, Cost-Saving Reforms		
GER1 = 110, GER2L = 60, GER2U = 30		Scenario 3
Primary	2,30%	47,9%
Lower Secondary	1,00%	20,8%
Upper Secondary	0,80%	16,7%
Upper Secondary	0,70%	14,6%
Total	4,80%	100,0%
GER1 = 110, GER2L = 100, GER2U = 50		Scenario 4
Primary	36,5%	36,5%
Lower Secondary	1,70%	27,0%
Upper Secondary	1,30%	20,6%
Other incl HE	0,90%	14,3%
Total	6,30%	100,0%

for primary and a total of 3,9% of GNP. To move from there to higher enrolment rates that should achieve UPE (GER1 = 110%) would require about 2,3% of GNP for primary at existing cost levels. However, if higher post-primary enrolment rates are to be achieved, the total needed would increase from 3,9% of GNP to 6% or 8,6%, depending on the levels of secondary enrolment targeted. With cost saving and efficiency reforms that reduced costs, 4,8% and 6,3% would be required.

Only in scenario 3 does primary allocation remain close to the benchmark of 50% for primary. This would require dramatic reductions in average unit costs at secondary level, which may not be achievable. The other scenarios would see allocation to primary shrink relative to other levels, but would need considerable increases in total allocations to education. Thus the benchmark of 50% may have to be reconsidered in the light of the financial implications of expanded post-primary access and the specific contexts and priorities of different systems.

In conclusion
This article has explored the current status of education in relation to the EFA goals and MDGs, reflected on issues raised by the specification of the goals, drawn attention to needs to link policy and practice to the theoretical debates on the role of education in development, and invited reconceptualisation of access and equity issues drawing on the evidence base. It has argued that target setting and indicative benchmarks have a value but that they can also distort some aspects of the educational development process.

The thrust of this article is to reconsider how targets and benchmarks can be generated that are collectively owned through a process that embeds them in national policy debate, seeks to generate a consensus amongst key stakeholders and ownership by implementers, and derives from a relevant evidence base. To be useful, such targets and benchmarks need to be feasible over defined time periods, discussed with those with experience of implementation, linked to other targets and tested for consistency, and presented in forms that can be understood by key stakeholders at different levels of the education system. They must also result in financially sustainable outcomes.

It may also be useful to consider the value of targets and benchmarks focused on rates of improvement and distributional measures. The former allows progress to be profiled at challenging but not unrealistic levels. The latter addresses a key need neglected in much planning, which is that aggregate measures conceal pockets of exclusion and outlying values for key parameters. Yet 'the last 20%' are often the ones who are experiencing educational provision defined by conditions a standard deviation or more from the mean. In many SSA systems both access and quality would be considerably improved by reducing the variance between those in the core of the system and those at its margins.

References

Aikman, S and el Haj, H. (2005) Mobile multigrade schooling as a pragmatic response to EFA for pastoralist peoples. In Little, AW (ed.). *Education For All: The Challenge of Multigrade Teaching.* Amsterdam: Kluwer Academic Publishers.

Birdsall, N, Levine, R and Ibrahim, A. (2005) *Toward Universal Primary Education: Investments, Incentives and Institutions: Task Force on Achieving Universal Primary Education.* New York: United Nations Millennium Project.

Boyle, S, Brock, A, Mace, J and Sibbons, M. (2002) *Reaching the poor: The 'costs' of sending children to school: A six country study.* DFID Educational Papers No. 47. London: DFID.

Bruns, B, Mingat, A and Raktomalala, R. (2003) *A Chance for Every Child: Achieving Universal Primary Education by 2015.* Washington: World Bank.

Buchmann, C and Brakewood, D. (2000) Labor Structures and School Enrollments in Developing Societies: Thailand and Kenya Compared. *Comparative Education Review,* 44(2): 175-204.

Canagarajah, S and Nielsen, H. (1999) *Child labor and schooling in Africa: A comparative study.* Social Protection Discussion Paper Series No. 9916. Washington: World Bank.

Chowdhury, AMR, Nath, SR and Choudhury, RK. (2003) Equity gains in Bangladesh primary education. *International Review of Education,* 49(6): 601-619.

Colclough, C, Al-Samarrai, S, Rose, P and Tembon, M. (2003) *Achieving Schooling for All in Africa: Costs, Commitment and Gender.* Aldershot and Burlington: Ashgate.

Colclough, C with Lewin, KM. (1993) *Educating All the Children; Strategies for Primary Education in Developing Countries.* Oxford: Oxford University Press.

Daun, H. (2000) Primary education in sub-Saharan Africa – a moral issue, an economic matter, or both? *Comparative Education,* 36(1): 37-53.

Dunne, M and Leach, FE. (2005) *Gendered school experiences: The impact on retention and achievement in Botswana and Ghana.* DFID Educational Papers No. 54. London: DFID.

Fentiman, A, Hall, A and Bundy, D. (1999) School enrolment patterns in rural Ghana: A comparative study on the impact of location, gender, age and health on children's access to basic schooling. *Comparative Education*, 35(3): 331-349.

Kabeer, N, Nambissan, GB and Subrahmanian, R (eds). (2003) *Child Labour and the Right to Education in South Asia: Needs versus Rights?* New Delhi, Thousand Oaks, California and London: Sage Publications.

Laugharn, P. (2001) Negotiating 'education for many': Enrolment, dropout and persistence in the community schools of Kolondieba, Mali. Unpublished PhD thesis, University of London.

Lewin, KM. (2005) Taking targets to task: Planning post primary education. *International Journal of Education and Development* 25(4): 408-422.

Lewin, KM. (2006a) The Limits to Growth of Non-Government Schooling in Sub-Saharan Africa. In Walford, G and Srivastava, P. *Private Schools in Developing Countries.* Oxford: Symposium Books.

Lewin, KM. (2006b) Planning for secondary expansion in sub-Saharan Africa – key issues for sustainable growth in access. *Perspectives in Education* 24(2): 109-121.

Lewin, KM. (2006c) *Seeking Secondary Schooling in Sub-Saharan Africa: Strategies for Sustainable Financing.* Secondary Education in Africa (SEIA) (http://www.worldbank.org/afr/seia/) document. Washington DC: World Bank.

Lewin, KM. (2007) *Improving access, equity and transitions in education: Creating a research agenda.* CREATE Pathways to Access; Research Monograph No 1. University of Sussex: CREATE.

Lewin, KM and Caillods, F. (2001) *Financing Secondary Education in Developing Countries: Strategies for Sustainable Growth.* Paris: International Institute for Educational Planning.

Lewin, KM and Sayed, Y. (2005) *Non-government secondary schooling in sub-Saharan Africa: Exploring the evidence in South Africa and Malawi.* DFID Educational Paper (in press).

Lewin, KM and Stuart, JS. (2003) *Researching Teacher Education: New Perspectives on Practice, Performance and Policy.* DFID Educational Papers, No. 49. London: DFID.

Little, AW. (ed.). (2006) *Education For All and Multigrade Teaching: Challenges and Opportunities.* Dordrecht: Springer.

Little, AW. (1999) *Labouring to Learn: Towards a Political Economy of Plantations, People and Education in Sri Lanka.* London: Macmillan.

Mukudi, E. (2004) The effects of user-fee policy on attendance rates among Kenyan elementary school children. *International Review of Educa-*

tion, 50(5-6): 447-461.

Nokes, C, Van de Bosch, C and Bundy, DAP. (1998) *The Effects of Iron Deficiency and Anemia on Mental and Motor Performance, Educational Achievement, and Behavior in Children: An Annotated Bibliography.* INACG document. Washington, DC: ILSI Press.

Pridmore, P, Yates, C, Kuhn, K and Xerinda, H. (2005) *The role of open, distance and flexible learning (ODFL) in mitigating the impact of HIV/AIDS on out-of-school youth in South Africa and Mozambique.* DFID Educational Papers (in press).

Ravallion, M and Wodon, Q. (1999) Does child labor displace schooling? Evidence on behavioural responses to an enrolment subsidy. World Bank Policy Research Working Paper No 2116.

Rose, P and Al-Samarrai, S. (2001) Household constraints on schooling by gender: Empirical evidence from Ethiopia. *Comparative Education Review*, 45(1): 36-63.

UNESCO. (2000) *The Dakar Framework for Action. Education for All: Meeting our Collective Commitments.* Paris: UNESCO.

UNESCO. (2001) *EFA Global Monitoring Report 2002: Education for All – Is the world on track?* Paris: UNESCO.

UNESCO. (2003) *EFA Global Monitoring Report 2003/4: Gender and Education for All -The Leap to Equality.* Paris: UNESCO.

UNESCO. (2004) *EFA Global Monitoring Report 2005: Education for All – The Quality Imperative.* Paris: UNESCO.

UNESCO. (2005) *EFA Global Monitoring Report 2006: Education for All – Literacy for Life.* Paris: UNESCO.

United Nations (2000) The Millennium Development Goals. Website: http://www.un.org/millennium goals/

Education, skills, sustainability and growth: Complex relations[1]

Kenneth KING

Many developing countries since Jomtien in 1990, and more especially since Dakar in 2000, and the elaboration of the Millennium Development Goals (MDGs) later that same year, have seen international concern to assist them to reach the six Dakar targets. While there has been some very detailed work on analysing progress towards these Dakar Goals (e.g. the Global Monitoring Reports on Education for All – EFA), much less attention has been given to the sustainability of these externally-assisted achievements. Will countries that have been assisted to reach universal primary education be able to sustain this when development assistance is terminated? It is not therefore just a question of whether the world is on track to reach the Dakar Goals, but whether individual countries have an economic and political environment that will secure them. Intimately connected to that challenge is an assessment of what is available after school to the millions of young people who have been persuaded to enter and complete basic education. What has happened to the labour market environment, and especially to the nature of work in the widespread urban and rural informal economy, during the years that countries have been encouraged to focus on the achievement of the Dakar Goals?

Many developing countries since the World Conference on Education for All in Jomtien in 1990, and more especially since the Dakar World Forum on Education in 2000, and the elaboration of the Millennium Development Goals (MDGs) later that same year, have seen international concern to assist them to reach the six Dakar targets. While there has been some very thorough work on analysing progress towards these Dakar Goals (e.g. the Global Monitoring Reports on Education for All – EFA), much less attention has been given to the sustainability of these externally-assisted achievements. Will countries that have been assisted to reach universal primary education be able to sustain this when development assistance is terminated? It is not therefore just a question of whether the world is on track to reach the Dakar Goals, but whether individual countries have an economic and political environment that will continue to secure them. Intimately connected to that challenge is an assessment of what is available after school to the millions of young people who have been persuaded to enter and complete basic education. What has happened to the labour market environment, and especially to the nature of skills and of work in the widespread urban and rural informal economy, during the years that countries have been encouraged to focus on the achievement of the Dakar Goals?

As a consequence, in the sphere of technical and vocational skills development (TVSD), there has been a recognition that this sector has come back onto the agenda of development partners as well as of many national governments, especially in Asia and sub-Saharan Africa (NORRAG 2007; King and Palmer 2007). Arguably, however, there is a direct connection between the emphasis on EFA over the last 15 years and the re-emergence of TVSD. Policy-makers in aid agencies and in national governments have been aware that the very 'success' of EFA has been producing some of the largest cohorts of young school-leavers ever recorded in some countries, and this has generated an intense debate about 'Education for what?' as well as the role of skills provision as one response to the challenge. However, valuable though TVSD may be for school-leavers, it too is not a guarantee of work or of a job, in either the formal or the informal sector. There is no automatic connection amongst school, skill and work.

Policy attention has begun to shift, therefore, to an examination of what the enabling environments are in which EFA and TVSD can lead sustainably to poverty reduction and growth (Mayoux and Palmer 2007). If there is no change in the productivity of work in the informal sector, and if foreign direct investment remains miniscule for many developing countries, what will be the impact on families who have invested in the basic education and training of their children over this last decade and more? Will they sustain these investments for their younger children if school and skill do not lead to improved economic outcomes for the older ones?

This article addresses this question of whether the last 17 years since Jomtien have witnessed an element of unsustainable financing of education and training. Has there been insufficient attention, in the focus on the six Dakar Goals, on the wider investments in agriculture, industry and infrastructure that the Commission for Africa (2005) and the UN Millennium Project (2005) have argued are necessary accompaniments to the securing of the MDGs?

Evidence will be reviewed from a series of Asian countries, as well as from Africa. Some attention will be paid to China for the lessons that can perhaps be learnt for other countries from the 'development-oriented poverty reduction' in China's own poorer Western provinces (LGOP 2003).

It may be useful initially, however, to explore and clarify whether the current UN discourse about education for sustainable development, or about TVET, or literacy, for sustainable development, has any connection with our concerns here about sustainable financing for education and training. That discourse then needs to be related conceptually to the discourse on aid dependency, with its intimate connection to sustainable national financing of education, skills training and other social goals. And that in turn leads straight back to the issue of continued economic growth at the country level, which tends not to look at the character of this economic growth in terms of environmental sustainability. Thus it is suggested here that there is a set of key discourses that need to be connected (and interrogated) if any sense is to be made of the pursuit, simultaneously, of the MDGs on the one hand, raising the levels of aid for developing countries on the other, but also reducing aid dependency, by maintaining or increasing national levels of economic growth. It appears that the general term 'sustainable development' is often a convenient envelope that can actually contain a series of frequently conflicting goals, not least the pursuit of financial sustainability and environmental sustainability along with the EFA and MDG targets.

Education and training for sustainable development versus sustainable levels of education and training for development

As a result of the World Summit on Sustainable Development in Johannesburg in 2002, a Decade of Education for Sustainable Development (DESD) was declared from 2005 to 2014. UNESCO was requested to take leadership of this decade and to develop an implementation plan for it. There are four major thrusts to this discourse of education for sustainable development (ESD). These are:

- Improving access to quality basic education
- Reorienting existing education programmes
- Developing public understanding and awareness
- Providing training (UNESCO 2005: 7)

Since accepting this leadership obligation, UNESCO has indeed developed an international implementation plan (UNESCO 2005), and this document analyses the evolving notion of sustainable development. There are three core dimensions: environment, society and economy. In terms of our concern with sustainable economic growth in this present article, it might be expected that the implementation plan would address the nature of economic growth. Surprisingly, however, there is almost no mention of economic growth in the entire paper. In fact, economic issues are discussed only in relation to poverty reduction and to corporate social responsibility and accountability. There is no attempt to discuss either the need for national economic growth to make EFA (and TVSD) sustainable and to avoid long-term aid dependency, nor of the trade-offs between such economic growth and environmental sustainability.

Intriguingly, one of the peculiar characteristics of the ESD or DESD discourses is that they have a strong ethical tone to them. Thus, the implementation plan talks much more of values than of economic issues or of growth, while in the *Prospects* Open File on 'Education for sustainable development', the guest editor, G Lopez-Ospina, talks of 'sustainable development' being 'more a *moral precept* than a *scientific concept*, linked as much with notions of fairness as with theories of global warming'. He goes on to argue that sustainable development is 'primarily a matter of culture. It is connected with *values* people cherish and with the ways in which they perceive their relationships with others' (Lopez-Ospina 2000: 32-33).

Similarly, in a thoughtful discussion paper on 'Orienting technical and vocational education and training for sustainable development' by the UNESCO-UNEVOC Centre in Bonn, it is argued that 'sustainable development ... is primarily a matter of culture: it is concerned with the values people cherish and with the ways in which we perceive our relationships with others and with the natural world' (UNESCO-UNEVOC 2006: 5).

The UNEVOC paper does, however, also admit that technical and vocational education and training (TVET) is too often linked into 'productivism', providing skilled workers for industry, on the assumption of continued economic growth. The discussion paper argues, by contrast, that TVET can also be linked to economic literacy, sustainable production and sustainable consumption, but only with massive gains in technological efficiency and with the 'dematerialization of production and consumption' (*ibid*.16). However, the paper is more concerned with how TVET courses can build in awareness of sustainable development than with the financial sustainability of providing education and skills for all, as part of the developing world's bid for modernisation.

Education for All versus financial sustainability?

It is surprising that neither in this literature of ESD and DESD nor in other commentaries on sustainable development does the obvious tension between the sheer cost of reaching and maintaining education for all get much discussed in the same breath as sustainable development. For example, in the EFA Global Monitoring Report (GMR) for 2007, the following claim is made without any acknowledgement that there may be a tension between achieving universal education and sustainable development:

> Building on two United Nations instruments, the Universal Declaration of Human Rights and the Convention on the Rights of the Child, the international community adopted the Declaration on Education for All at Jomtien, Thailand, in 1990. At its heart is the recognition that universal education is the key to sustainable development, social justice and a brighter future. (UNESCO 2006: 13)

Perhaps not surprisingly, the Jomtien World Conference, coming one year before the Rio Summit, did not actually talk of sustainable development, but it did mention as part of its Framework for Action that 'development agencies should establish policies and plans for the 1990s, in line with their commitments to sustained, long-term support for national and regional actions ...' (World Conference 1990: 20). By the time of OECD-DAC articulation of the International Development Targets in 1996, however, there was not only a target specifically concerned with the securing of national strategies for sustainable development, but an acknowledgement that there was a 'broad range of less quantifiable factors of importance to sustainable development. These range from improved capacity for managing economic and social policies to heightened attention to issues of accountability, the rule of law and human rights, expanded participation and the accumulation of social capital and appreciation for environmental sustainability' (OECD-DAC 1996: 8). What is valuable about this comment is that sustainable development is distinguished from environmental sustainability.

Elsewhere in the EFA GMR for 2007, it is acknowledged, in a single, brief paragraph, that there may indeed be a problem where aid contributes a substantial share of the education (or basic education) budget. For example, for the 20 country plans thus far endorsed by the Fast Track Initiative (FTI), on average one-quarter of the costs will need to be covered by external aid. More worryingly, it was estimated in 2002 by the World Bank that to cover the financing gap for reaching universal primary education by 2015 'aid would need to reach an average of 42 per cent of total expenditure on primary education and much more in some countries' (UNESCO 2006: 98). In other words, very substantial amounts of external funding would be needed in such countries, if the education MDGs were to be reached. What is also acknowledged, however, is the volatility and unpredictability of this external aid. In other words, the likely unsustainability of aid flows is admitted.

So we have an interesting anomaly, apparently; the literature on education for sustainable development pays little attention to the sustainability of educational achievements, which have, in some cases, been made possible by large amounts of rather unpredictable educational aid. This ESD literature seems more interested in how education and training at different levels can assist in transmitting messages about sustainable development than in the sustainability of national educational ambitions. On the other hand, the EFA literature on reaching the education MDGs seems much more preoccupied with raising the aid volumes to facilitate this process than with looking at the sustainability issues involved in reaching the MDGs on the back of external resources. It might have been thought that what we might call a sustainable development approach to the MDGs would have been highly appropriate, since it is clear that reaching the MDGs is not a one-year Olympiad in 2015, but a process that needs eventually to be sustained on local resources. However, the actual MDG 7, which is directly concerned with ensuring environmental sustainability, does not itself address any of the complexity linked to the financial sustainability of the MDG process itself; it merely promotes the idea 'to integrate the principles of sustainable development into country policies and programmes; reverse loss of environmental resources' along with reducing by half the numbers without access to safe drinking water, and improving the lives of at least 100 million slum dwellers.[2]

We should not under-estimate the complex mix of factors that need to be borne in mind if education, skills and sustainable development are to be satisfactorily discussed. Thus we shall first analyse the situation with a lens on education, and then include discussion on training and skills development. We shall find that it is not sufficient to talk about financing gaps, but rather that a series of other factors, including country level commitment, economic growth, the enabling environment and aid dependency, to mention just a few, must be considered.

Sustainable approaches to the Dakar Goals and the education MDGs via growth?

In the most recent EFA Global Monitoring Report – that for 2007 – we have already noted the claim that universal primary education is the key to sustainable development. But a closer examination of the argument suggests there was an awareness in the GMR team of just how many factors needed to be considered in arguing for priority for the Dakar Goals.

For one thing, if the price tag for the achievement of the EFA agenda is really as high as US$11 billion a year as argued by the GMR 2007 (UNESCO 2006: 102), then the share of basic education in total EFA in low-income countries would need to more than double if there is to be sustained progress towards the goals. But it is not just a question of making the case to donors, many of whom have been relatively well disposed, in principle at least, towards higher aid budgets since Gleneagles in 2005. As the GMR 2007 admits, there is also more competition for new aid money. Increasingly, aid donors and national governments are aware that the predominantly social expenditures associated with the Dakar and MDG targets need to be accompanied by more attention to infrastructure investments, if the expenditure on social spending is to be sustainable. This thinking has come in part from the Commission for Africa and the Millennium Project Report, but certain donors, notably Japan, now joined by China, and once again the World Bank (2006), have been urging more attention to infrastructure development. We shall look briefly at some of these accounts of the needs for massive growth in investment in infrastructure if social goals and achievements are to be sustained.

Both the Millennium Project Report and the Commission for Africa broke new ground by insisting that increased growth rates and investment would be required if the MDGs were to be secure. Indeed, the Commission for Africa has argued strongly (in its chapter on 'Going for Growth and Poverty Reduction') that Africa needed to reach an average growth rate of seven per cent and sustain it, if all the closely linked other investments (including social) are to be secured and sustained. But the Commission is also clear that this economic growth target needs to be associated with a strong attachment to the three goals of sustainable development: economic, social and environmental (Commission for Africa 2005: 219, 248). In particular there was an emphasis on the requirement that 'sustainable economic growth' involve 'prudent use of natural resources and effective protection of the environment' (*ibid*). It was also sure that substantially increased aid would be required to help initially achieve this crucial level of economic growth.

Recent World Bank thinking on the complex connections amongst education investment, sustainable growth and other enabling factors supports the stance taken by the Millennium Project Report and also the Commission for Africa. UPE is just the 'beginning step for survival in today's complex, fast-globalizing world' (World Bank 2005: 47). What it terms 'education for dynamic economies' is equally a requirement to increase productivity and sustain growth. This enlarged vision is a very welcome addition to the Bank's education agenda, and it should be noted that 'financial sustainability' is included as one of the inter-sectoral issues that cannot be secured by focusing on development through a single lens such as education investment:

> Rather than concentrate on a particular level of education, it emphasizes a holistic approach that not only addresses needs at all levels, but, indeed, recognizes that the challenges of access, equity, education quality, efficiency, financial sustainability, and governance and management are intra-sectoral issues that will never be adequately understood and addressed if they are considered from the perspective of education levels. (World Bank 2005: 48).

It should be noted that the language of 'financial sustainability' is much more acceptable than 'aid dependency'.[3] (In certain agencies, it is known that employees have been actively discouraged from talking openly about aid dependency, as it might discourage donors from increasing their aid.) The ambition in the Commission for Africa and the Millennium Project Report dramatically to increase aid, especially to Africa, has naturally raised concerns about what it actually means for a country to reach the MDGs on the back of external aid.[4] Aid dependency is not a popular topic in a world that is expected to assist poorer countries in reaching the MDGs; and hence the term *aid dependency* does not get much attention in any of these three reports. The Commission for Africa, under the heading 'Is extra aid forever?', does briefly address the challenge of aid recipients becoming permanently reliant on aid. But the Commission's strong position is that, from South Korea to Botswana, aid has been shown to be able actively to assist the transformation from being a recipient to a successful middle-income country. Their view, not dissimilar from the Millennium Project Report, is that there needs to be a sufficiently large 'big push' from external assistance to help kick-start the growth process. 'Where the growth process succeeds, aid tapers out.' It is only when national reform efforts, supported externally, are too small that they fear that the 'world will be faced with a permanent aid programme to Africa' (Commission for Africa 2005: 327).

The World Bank, in a somewhat parallel perspective, conceives that in the poorest countries of Africa, performance-based aid can play a role in giving the political space for reforms, but this may imply 'high aid dependency for a sustained period of time' (World Bank 2005: 56). This open-ended commitment for many years must be a concern to many donors, even if the MDGs are seen as a minimum standard that needs to be reached, regardless of dependency. Some analysts worry that for external bodies, in effect, to be paying the teachers' salaries of poorer countries is essentially unsustainable, not just because of the unpredictability of aid and the frequent political role of teacher lobbies, but because these investments do not alter the wider macro-economic environment that is ultimately needed to sustain such payments.

Reaching and securing the MDGs: A sustainability challenge

Compared with the enormous international effort put into calculating progress towards the MDGs and their specific indicators (e.g. United Nations 2007) and the estimation of what nations are 'on track' to reach the six Dakar Goals in education and which are not (through the EFA Global Monitoring Reports), it could be argued that a good deal more attention than at present might have gone into analysing the sustainability of national education and skills development systems more generally.[5] These systems, at secondary, vocational and tertiary levels, have in fact been directly affected, especially in economically weaker and more dependent countries, by the international preoccupation with the MDGs and the Dakar Goals.[6] This is a little-recognised additional impact of aid dependency.

But the impact of the international agenda-setting around EFA since Jomtien and Dakar is not only to be measured in terms of agency shifts in aid priorities; the focus on the Dakar Goals and on the MDGs has also affected in some measure even those countries that were much less aid-dependent. The result, arguably, has been very much larger cohorts coming through primary than ever before. This, in turn, has created massive political pressure to expand both lower secondary (often said to be part of the basic cycle of education) and upper secondary This expansion has often been carried out with inadequate national financing, whether at secondary, vocational or tertiary levels. But the results of the entitlement agenda around basic education are the creation of a very large group of young people whose aspirations for work at a certain level have been lifted by completing full primary education, but for whom opportunities in the national economy have changed very little. Compared with the huge international preoccupation with the MDGs and Dakar Goals, with their focus on the supply side of the future workforce, much less attention has been given to the creation of new productive capacities in the developing world, with the exception of the ILO's 'Decent Work for All' agenda, UNCTAD's least developed countries report (UNCTAD, 2006), and the Commission for Africa's emphasis on 'Going for Growth' and 'More Trade' (Commission for Africa 2005: chapters 7 and 8).

In fact, it could be said that the EFA and MDG agendas are predominantly supply-side; whereas in the last 10 years vocational educators and planners have become used to thinking seriously about the demand-side. There is of course an inherent tension in the rights-based supply-side thinking associated with meeting the goals or the targets for basic education, and the demand-led thinking now so widely associated with the planning of TVSD.

The only parallel in the last 40 to 50 years to the massive supply-side initiatives since Jomtien was the expansion, especially in sub-Saharan Africa, of education systems (at all levels) in the immediate pre-and post-independence period. Then at least there were a significant number of new jobs created in the burgeoning ministries and through Africanisation of former European positions. But in this most recent expansion, there has been little corresponding job creation. In many countries, EFA expansion has been accompanied by jobless growth. Whatever the virtues of the universal access to basic education – and few would dispute this entitlement agenda – there is something inherently unsustainable about expecting poor countries (and poor families) to continue to invest in basic education when there is no corresponding work available, beyond what can be found in the informal economy (King 2005).

The dilemma of sub-Saharan Africa's abundant labour supply (fuelled in part by external aid for reaching EFA) and minimal labour market demand has been set out very sharply by Fredriksen, former senior education advisor for sub-Saharan Africa in the World Bank:

As regards post-basic education, I see a real problem in most African countries where –

1. on the (labour) supply side there is a very rapid increase in supply of youth with some primary and/or secondary education, driven by a combination of continued rapid population growth and rapid increase in intake and survival in primary education; and

2. on the (labour market) demand side, a tiny modern sector (an almost non-existent manufacturing sector in most African countries) and limited possibility for creation of modern-sector jobs (outside extractive industries) owing, inter alia, to a lack of competitiveness of these countries vis-à-vis China, Vietnam and other countries on export markets as a result of factors like comparatively high labour costs and a very poor business environment that does not attract direct foreign investment.

> In fact, I would argue that there has probably never been a region in the world where the gap between, respectively, supply and demand for 'educated' labour was larger than in sub-Saharan Africa today (with the exception of a few countries). How they can reach the high level of growth needed to address this growing youth unemployment problem over the next two to three decades is for me a difficult problem. (Fredriksen 2007)

Fredriksen points to the growth challenge presented by these uniquely large numbers of young people exiting basic education. From one international perspective, these numbers are part of a success story, as they constitute success on the EFA Development Index (see UNESCO 2006: 196); but from another, they present a huge political problem. Aid has helped to create this EFA success in countries such as Ghana, and many others. But what of the famous connection between aid and high growth rates that we were discussing above in relation to the Commission for Africa? Has Africa's economic growth in the last decade and more begun to change the economic and labour market environment that these young people will confront?

The paradox of successful growth, but with little poverty reduction and few jobs

One of the apparent success stories in Africa has been persistently high levels of economic growth in recent years. For instance, Ghana has experienced growth in the four to five per cent range over more than 20 years, and was forecast to reach 6,5 per cent in 2007 (Palmer 2007: 1). The IMF reported in 2005 that the number of African countries reaching five per cent growth had hit a record high of 20 nations with inflation of less than ten per cent.

However, the IMF has also warned that these economies are still not growing fast enough to reduce poverty levels, and that their business environments are still not friendly enough (BBC News 2007). Similarly, the United Nations Economic Commission for Africa has acknowledged that 'Africa's real GDP grew by 4,6 per cent in 2004, the highest in almost a decade, up from 4,3 per cent in 2003. ... [this] reflects a continued upward trend since 1998. Unfortunately, the growth has so far not been translated to employment creation or poverty reduction' (Africa Focus 2005). But are bodies like the Commission for Africa really saying that if only the growth rate were seven per cent instead of five per cent, then all the positive effects would be gained? No, they are claiming that growth must indeed rise to seven per cent by 2010, but that it must be growth in which poor people can participate. In other words, a growth rate that is driven merely by higher oil and commodity prices is very different from growth that derives from a series of strategic investments in infrastructure, agriculture and the creation of a climate that fosters development (Commission for Africa 2005: 251).

It could in fact be argued that these new, higher growth rates for much of Africa have been positively assisted by India and particularly China's search for oil and other commodities in the continent. But what Western analysts and agencies seem to be saying is that the growth rates not only need to be maintained and increased, but that parallel reforms need to be undertaken to make the investment and business environment more attractive as well as ensuring the participation of poor people in the benefits of growth. For example, in Ghana these are precisely the reforms that the government has been undertaking:

The government is in the process of implementing other strategies aimed at stimulating growth and development, for example in: infrastructure, ICT, science/technology and health. Indeed, these kind of parallel strategies appear to be in line with much of the international literature regarding the need for large multi-sectoral investments to kick-start sustainable development (e.g. Commission for Africa, UN Millennium Project). (Palmer 2007: 15)

But there is, in fact, a kind of catch 22 in Africa's pursuit of development via the MDGs and the Dakar targets. The continent has been urged to reach these, but it has been acknowledged that these goals and targets are pre-eminently social investments with little specified in the way of strengthening Africa's productive capacities. Hence if countries are to develop a sustainable infrastructure and economic base to maintain their achievement of these social goals, they not only need a solid revenue base, but they need to demonstrate to their peoples that investment in six to seven years of basic education for all their children does have a clear economic and labour market pay-off. This may already not be the case today. What may well happen is that the pressure to provide some form of post-basic education to the most vocal (i.e. middle-class and urban populations) will mean that a substantial proportion of the primary age cohort, especially rural girls, handicapped and orphans, will not be covered by basic education, or will eventually withdraw if they ever entered this level.

For there are two dimensions of sustainability related to the achievement of these goals and targets: one is economic, and relates to the national capacity to continue to fund the provision of EFA. The second, however, is equally vital, and could be termed attitudinal sustainability. It relates to the sustained commitment of the people to send all their children to school. This will not happen without it being evident that basic education is of a quality standard and that it can lead somewhere, either to higher levels of work or of post-basic schooling and skills training.

EFA, post-basic education and training (PBET) and their enabling and sustaining economic environments

Our criticism, therefore, of the role of international agencies in the construction of the global education agenda that has held sway for 15 years and more, since Jomtien in 1990, is not of course that it has diverted attention to basic education from other levels of education and training.[7]

A focus on the right of all children to basic education, even in the poorest countries in the developing world, was long overdue. Rather, it has been with the lack of attention to the conditions needed to sustain EFA in these poorer countries. One aspect of this crucial, enabling environment is within the education and training system itself, and involves seeing basic education as one part of a necessarily holistic system of post-basic education and training. A second dimension is the role of the macro-economic environment in supporting the education and training system (but also in part being dynamised by the quality of the education and training system).[8]

Currently we lack adequate accounts of how EFA and PBET are crucially affected by the wider macro-economic environment, and how they in turn can have a direct impact on that environment. China could provide one set of insights into this two-way process. One part of this account would be how China, through its nation-wide campaign for nine-year schooling, moved from a situation where the per capita coverage of education in the workforce was just 4,3 years of schooling on average prior to 1985 to a situation in 2001 where the average per capita years of schooling was 8,1. This, of course, had a major impact on the capacities of China's workforce, but this extraordinary achievement was also dynamised and motivated by the opening up of China to the world and the creation of a climate of new opportunities in work and in enterprise. Nor should it be forgotten that China has for 20 years sought to ensure that as near as possible to 50 per cent of its upper secondary cohort should enter vocational secondary schools.

China's approach to poverty reduction affords a fascinating insight into this two-way interaction between educational and scientific provision on the one hand, and investment in productive capacity on the other. Its 'Development-Oriented Poverty Reduction Programme' gives a flavour of China's national development strategy. It is interesting to note their use of the words 'holistic' and 'comprehensive' and to note how it parallels the assumptions made, two years later, by the Commission for Africa.

> First, stick to the comprehensive exploitation and all-round development. As cause for poverty is complicated (*sic*), so are the holistic measures for alleviating poverty. We must include the development-oriented poverty alleviation in the national economic

and social plan so that we can have a favourable external condition for the task. We must intensify our effort to build water conservancy, transportation, electricity, and communication infrastructures in order to contribute to the development of the poor areas and the poverty alleviation and a better life. It is necessary for the poor areas not only to develop production, increase farmers' incomes, but also pay attention to the development of science and technology, education, health care and culture, improve the community environment, raise the quality of life and propel a harmonious development and all round progress. Only in doing so, can we eradicate the poverty at its root. (LGOP 2003: 98-99)

Currently, a series of other countries, including India, Pakistan and Ghana, are being looked at in ways that would allow some consideration of how the provision and impact of skills training programmes also need to take account of the wider economic, social and political environment. Instead of a solely education-centric or training-centric approach, these two-way research approaches hope to show that the impact of education and training systems is inseparable from the environments in which they are embedded. This is not a deterministic position, because, as has been argued above, the character, quality and extent of education and training systems also have an influence on these surrounding environments.

It may be useful to close with a listing of just a few areas where 'going for growth' needs to be rethought much more carefully in relation to sustainable education and training systems.

Provisional propositions on the multiple dimensions of education, skill and sustainability

- The UN and UNESCO discourses around 'Education and Training for Sustainable Development' are highly edu-centric; they expect education and training to raise awareness of sustainable development. But they have thus far paid little attention to the sustainability of the systems of education and training themselves.
- The EFA and MDG discourses also seem to pay relatively little

attention to the differential national capacity to sustain the achievement of the Dakar Goals or the MDGs, even when securing these is heavily dependent on external aid. Aid dependency is little discussed in these discourses, since the emphasis has often been on the need to increase external aid dramatically rather than review the dangers of its volatility and unpredictability.

- The Commission for Africa and the UN Millennium Project discourses assume a virtuous relationship between substantial, long-term aid flows and a certain rather high level of GDP growth (by OECD standards) – seven per cent. In this thinking, aid is assumed to be able to play a key role in kick-starting a pattern of sustainable growth.

- Inadequate attention has been given to several sustainability dimensions of the relationship between education and skills development, on the one hand, and their surrounding environments, on the other. Such evidence as we have of the crucial two-way relationships between education and training and their enabling (or indeed disabling) environments would suggest that further research would throw valuable light on how the aspirations of young people and their families to stick with basic and post-basic education and training are connected to this wider economic context.

These few propositions suggest that theoretically we have a long way to go in understanding the complex interactions amongst education, skills and sustainable growth.

References

Africa Focus. (2005) Africa: Economic growth improving. Available at www.africafocus.org/docs05/eca0505.php [accessed 6 September 2007].

BBC News. (2007) Africa hits record growth – IMF. Available at http://news.bbc.co.uk/2/hi/africa/4447773.stm [accessed 6 September 2007].

Commission for Africa (2005) *Our Common Interest: Report of the Commission for Africa*. London: DFID.

Fredriksen, B. (2007) Personal communication to K King, 27 August 2007.

King, K. (2004a) Development knowledge and the global policy agenda. Whose Knowledge? Whose Policy? Paper to Conference on Social

Knowledge and International Policy-Making: Can Research Make a Difference? UNRISD, Geneva, 20-21 April 2004.

King, K. (2004b) The external agenda of educational reform: A challenge to educational self-reliance and dependency in sub-Saharan Africa. *Journal of International Cooperation in Education,* 7(1), April 2004: 83-96.

King, K. (2005) Re-targeting schools, skills and jobs in Kenya: Quantity, quality and outcomes. *International Journal of Educational Development,* 25(1): 423-435.

King, K. (2007a) Multilateral agencies in the construction of the global agenda on education. *Comparative Education,* 43(3), August 2007: 321-336.

King, K. (2007b) Higher education and international cooperation. In Stephens, D (ed). *Higher Education and Capacity Building: Celebration of 25 Years of the Higher Education Links Programme.* Oxford: Symposium Books.

King, K and Palmer, R. (2007) *Technical and Vocational Skills Development: A DFID briefing paper.* London: DFID.

LGOP (Leading Group Office of Poverty Alleviation and Development). (2003) *An Overview of the Development-Oriented Poverty Reduction Programme for Rural China.* Beijing: China Financial and Economic Publishing House.

Lopez-Ospina, G. (2000) Education for sustainable development: A local and international challenge. *Prospects,* XXX(1), March 2000: 31-40.

Mayoux, L and Palmer, R. (2007 forthcoming) *The Role of Skills Development in Creating a New Cycle of Opportunity for the Poor: Impact and Lessons from Developing Countries.* Geneva: ILO.

NORRAG. (2007) *NORRAG NEWS No 38: Special Issue on Technical and Vocational Skills Development.* University of Hong, China, February 2007 (www.norrag.org).

OECD-DAC (1996) *Shaping the 21st Century: The Contribution of Development Cooperation.* Paris: OECD, DAC.

Palmer, R. (2007) Technical and vocational skills development and impressive economic growth: Policy and research challenges for Ghana. Paper for the 9th UKFIET International Conference on Education and Development: Going for Growth? School, Community, Economy, Nation. Oxford, UK, 11-13 September 2007.

Palmer, R, Wedgwood, R, Hayman, R, King, K, Thin, N. (2007) *Educating out of Poverty? A Synthesis Report on Ghana, India, Kenya, Rwanda, Tanzania and South Africa.* DFID Researching the Issues Series No.

70. London: DFID (available through the DFID Website).

Penrose, P. (1993) *Planning and Financing Sustainable Education Systems in Sub-Saharan Africa.* Education Research Serial No. 7. London: Overseas Development Administration.

Sida. (1996) *Aid Dependency: Causes, Symptoms and Remedies.* Project 2015. Stockholm: Sida.

UNCTAD. (2006) *Developing Productive Capacities: The Least Developed Countries Report 2006.* Geneva: UNCTAD.

UNESCO. (2005) *International Implementation Plan: United Nations Decade of Education for Sustainable Development, 2005-2014.* Paris: UNESCO.

UNESCO. (2006) *Strong Foundations: Early Childhood Care and Education. EFA Global Monitoring Report 2007.* Paris: UNESCO.

UNESCO-UNEVOC. (2006) Orienting technical and vocational education and training for sustainable development. Discussion Paper No. 1, UNEVOC, Bonn.

UN Millennium Project. (2005) *Investing in Development: A Practical Plan to Reach the Millennium Development Goals.* London: Earthscan.

United Nations. (2007) *The Millennium Development Goals Report 2007.* New York: United Nations.

World Bank. (2005) *Education Sector Strategy Update: Achieving Education for All, Broadening our Perspective, Maximizing our Effectiveness.* Washington: World Bank.

World Bank. (2006) Rethinking infrastructure for development. Annual Bank Conference on Development Economics, Tokyo, 29-30 May 2007.

World Conference on Education for All. (1990) *Framework For Action: Meeting Basic Learning Needs* (Guidelines for implementing the World Declaration on Education for All. On-line at http://www.unesco.org/education/efa/ed_for_all/background/07Bpubl.shtml.

---

[1] An earlier version of this article was presented at the 9th UKFIET International Conference on Education and Development: Going for Growth? School, Community, Economy, Nation. Oxford, 11-13 September 2007.

[2] For a statement of MDG Goal 7 on environmental sustainability, its three associated targets and the seven associated indicators, see the UN's MDG website, http://mdgs.un.org/unsd/mdg/Host.aspx?Content=Indicators/OfficialList.htm. The indicators do not tackle the nature of the growth needed at the country level.

[3] A valuable discussion of aid dependency can be found in Sida 1996.

[4] See King 2004a and 2004b for a discussion of Africa's 'welfare states'.

[5] For a very early, critical discussion of the 'expansionary approaches such as those of the Jomtien Conference which commit countries to build their education systems up further on weak foundations' see Penrose (1993: 26).

[6] For a discussion of their impact on higher education, for example, see King 2007a.

[7] On the role of multilateral agencies in the construction of the global agenda for education, see King 2007a.

[8] See Palmer et al (2007) for a discussion of these two interacting dimensions of the sustaining environment for EFA.

The developmental state in Africa

Dani W. NABUDERE

This article places the failure of higher education to transform the societies and economies of Africa within a broader analysis of the failures of post-independence states to achieve development, modernisation and nation-building. It describes how in response to these problems higher education has come to rely increasingly on commerce and business, and has lost focus on the interests and possible contributions of other social actors, notably the poor and marginalised. It describes how the failure of the developmental policies of post-independence states – inevitable in view of the historically-determined power relations of the time – opened the door for the imposition of neo-liberal policies, which however only increased the woes of African populations. Using the concept of the 'glocal', which recognises the power of the new technologies that link the world in a complex network, while also pointing to the energies of local cultures and economies, the article goes on to suggest how frequently marginalised informal economies, the cultural resources of the continent and the often substantial capital locked up in institutions such as pension funds could be mobilised to form new federal states from below. In this envisaged context, higher education and research, among other areas, could come into their own in the service of these newly energised African societies.

Introduction

When African countries rid themselves of European colonial domination, most post-colonial governments invested heavily in education at all levels, particularly in higher education, placing it at the centre of the national project of social advancement and development. Ministries of education were given the task of formulating educational policies and programmes aimed at producing people equipped with the skills and

95

knowledge necessary for the realisation of 'national development' and 'nation-building'. According to Dr Alex A Kwampong, the former vice-chancellor of the University of Ghana, African universities came into being at the same time or soon after the birth of the new African states. They were consciously conceived and designed by the new African leadership with their former colonial advisers as 'prime instruments' for the consolidation of independence. Therefore, in addition to serving the universal and basic objectives of universities everywhere, these universities were expected, above all, to promote the development and modernisation of their various countries along Western lines in the process of 'nation-building'. According to Kwampong, they were meant to be 'development universities,' playing much the same role as the land-grant colleges of the United States in the nineteenth century. Forty years on, however, African universities and the governments that created them have failed dismally to chart new paths for Africa's emancipation and liberation. Consequently, Africa finds itself in deep, multi-faceted crises that require deeply thought-out solutions and responses, if African rebirth is ever to be achieved (Vilakazi 1999: 205-206).

Currently, investment in higher education and research are becoming increasingly interfaced with the economic activities of companies. This in turn is creating new problems of relevance for universities as institutions of research and learning for the entire community. Their historical role of addressing the needs of society as a whole is being undermined. They cannot play a role as 'developmental universities' when they are forced to ignore the role played by other actors in society. In this new situation, both governments and industry are being called upon to take new responsibilities in shaping the policies of universities to this end.

In this new environment, investment in education comes to consist of universities playing the role of self-financing institutions with limited state support, but dependent increasingly on the private sector. In 'producing and distributing' knowledge in this way, the future university will be required to a great extent to sell its products – knowledge – in order to finance itself. But this is happening in a world where there is quick turnover and rapid obsolescence in knowledge production. This has highlighted the importance of tacit knowledge and other forms of knowledge that are produced outside the universities. Learning has become an ongoing process in a 'knowledge society' where knowledge itself becomes commoditised in a 'learning economy'.

We would like to suggest at this stage that a complete revamp of educational policy is needed as regards investment in education. This suggests a more grass-roots 'learning economy' approach that responds to local needs and a culturally relevant 'knowledge economy' that is flexible enough to accommodate the pressures emanating from the global economy but at the same time is rooted in the solutions embedded in tacit knowledge and social capital within communities and local entities. In short, we are calling for the recognition of emerging glocal markets, the glocal state and glocal civil society in an overarching new glocal society. We use the concept 'glocalization' to mean that we are living in an emerging globality in which local actors operating in local spaces become visible and important. This new phenomenon is encapsulated in the maxim: Thinking Globally and Acting Locally.

In this connection, we have to go beyond the debates about the need for a 'developmental state'. These have re-surfaced as a result of the collapse of the 'Washington Consensus' and the failure of the much-touted neo-liberal reorganisation of the global economy in most of the countries of the South where neo-liberal prescriptions were applied universally without regard to differing conditions. As is well known, the neo-liberal response was premised on the alleged failure of the 'developmental state' to play a key role in organising investments, apportioning credit through monetary and fiscal policies and cooperating with national capitalists to advance development in a globalising world. The neo-liberal prescriptions, however, undermined the very basis of a 'developmental state' as a response to under-development and intensified the gap between the very rich and the very poor in the world.

What is the 'developmental state'?

The 'developmental state' is in fact the very basis of capitalist development in the metropolitan centres, where capitalism emerged in its 'pure' form. This recognition arises from the Marxist analysis of the state and the rise of capitalism, its organisation, management and expansion. For Karl Marx, the state arises out of the class struggle and in the capitalist era, as in all eras of class society, the ruling class and state are inseparable. Thus the capitalist state in its essence with the bourgeoisie at its head is a developmental state, since the state must enhance the interests of capital as a whole, not a fraction of it. As Herring has observed:

> The successful developmental state, with historical irony, is one able to function as if it were the executive committee of the bourgeoisie. The question then may be more under what conditions we get a developmental *business class* than why we get a developmental state that will give capital its head – the original Marxist formula for success. (Herring 1999: 33; emphasis in the original)

The concept of the developmental state was crafted by Chalmers Johnson in relation to the Japanese experience of industrial development after the Second World War (Johnson 1999), an experience replicated in the so-called Four Tigers in South-East Asia. This led to the rethinking of the role of the state in the development process and the replicability of their policies and experiences in other developing countries. The lessons drawn from these experiences differed from country to country, shaped by particular conditions. However, in drawing lessons from these experiences, the specificity and multiplicity of the 'Four Tigers' experiences tended to be subsumed under generalised neo-liberal concepts as though they were 'pure' examples of the superiority of essentially laissez-faire policies. Specifically, reliance on market forces and the adoption of market-driven export-oriented development strategies were said to have led to efficient exploitation of the comparative advantage of these countries' cheap labour.

In fact, it was the combination of cultural and political factors in the crafting of state policy that contributed to the success of what can be called the Asian developmental states. Manuel Castells has noted that East Asian economies are based on formal and informal economic organisations that have different cultural elements. He identifies three 'cultural areas' in this respect: the Japanese communitarian approach, the Korean patrimonial logic and the Taiwanese patrilineal logic. He argues that the similarities and differences of these networks can be traced back to the cultural and institutional characteristics of the different societies. These cultures have intermixed over centuries and are deeply permeated by the philosophical and religious values of Confucianism and Buddhism, in their various national patterns. In these cultures, the basic unit of organisation is the family, not the individual, as in most African societies (Castells 2000: 195).

Castells further observes that the fundamental difference between the three cultures concerns the role of the state 'both historically and in the process of industrialization'. In all these cases, he notes, the state 'pre-empted civil society' so that both the merchant and industrial elites came under its guidance. But even then, he observes, in each case the state was historically different and played a different role. In analysing the contemporary role of the state, therefore, he correctly draws a distinction between the role of the state in history and the performance of the contemporary development state. In this way he observes that Japanese business groups and areas of Japanese influence were organised 'vertically around a core corporation with direct access to the state. This was very different with the Chinese state, which had very different relationships to business, especially in the Southern region – the fundamental source of Chinese entrepreneurship. In the case of China, the state did not act to guide the entrepreneurs and create markets. Instead the families did it on their own, bypassing the state and embedding market mechanism in socially constructed networks' (ibid: 196-197). This was also the case in Taiwan and Hong Kong. The African experience is quite different, requiring nuanced study.

In summary, the Asian developmental state was defined by both its class structure and the state's economic policy. In terms of the class structure of the bourgeoisie and the labouring classes, it was closely allied to business but able to maintain the autonomy needed to drive development of new industries. It maintained mass support through a combination of nationalist rhetoric and substantial improvements in the living standards of the workers and small businesspeople. This was associated with rapidly increasing employment and paternalistic labour relations in larger companies. Secondly, in terms of economic policy, the state intervened heavily to develop new industries, using a combination of massive amounts of subsidised credit with strong tariff protection, substantial training and infrastructure development. South Korea and Taiwan imitated the Japanese approach in establishing light-industrial exporting under multi-year plans, guided by a strong state.

In examining recent development experiences, such as those in South Africa, we have to include a much broader understanding of development and the role the state must play in this 'late capitalist' era. Amartya Sen (1999), in his *Development as Freedom,* suggested that development requires not only economic transformation, but also a process of expanding freedoms that people enjoy. He argues further that development requires the removal of major sources of unfreedom such as poverty as well as tyranny, poor economic opportunities and social deprivation, neglect of public facilities and intolerance or over-activity of repressive states. These broader definitions introduce qualitative aspects in the determination of the developmental state missing in the model articulated by Johnson in respect of Japan and other South Eastern states.

The African 'developmental state'?

These broader definitions of the developmental state indicate that African development was far from achievable from the beginning of continental decolonisation. The African post-colonial 'developmental state' was circumscribed by the colonial strategies intended to dismember and destroy pre-colonial African states. This destruction had the effect of disorienting Africans ontologically and epistemologically, rendering Africa more completely dependent on the colonial powers that dismantled the African world than was the case in Asia. Africa's colonial nation-building and state-building ventures were therefore characterised by continued domination from outside, because African political elites failed to consolidate nation-states beyond their colonial boundaries or even to integrate the people within them into nations. This signalled the failure of the pan-African idea of a federated united states of Africa.

African people were arguably subjected to a harsher colonial rule, preceded by the slave trade, than that in Asia and the Middle East. The drive to preserve and/or destroy African states and cultures became the dominant colonial preoccupation in later European colonisation beginning around the 1880s. There was a cultural component to the colonisation process, in the form of cultural imperialism that incorporated racist ideas that were much more comprehensively elaborated, and inserted in policies and institutions of racial discrimination, than was the case with the earlier colonies in Asia and Latin America. The result was that Africa became disjointed culturally, geographically and linguistically. Thus the kind of development initiated on the continent continued to be a carbon copy of that undertaken by the colonial states that independent Africa inherited. Hence we can indeed legitimately refer to 'post-colonial states.'

Basil Davidson has referred to the 'curse of the nation-state', which he sees as the 'Black Man's Burden' (Davidson 1992). It was truly so. Indeed, 'nation-building' was, in the British case, a policy they had embarked on to bring their African possessions to self-government and ultimately to independence. According to Sir Hilton Poynton, the former administrative head of the British Colonial Office, the political and development agenda encapsulated in nation-building meant 'building separate nation-states as the successors and inheritors of the colonial state' (Davidson 1992: 168-170). Increased anti-colonial resistance prompted this strategy. The period was also characterised by a fevered attempt to increase bureaucratisation of the colonial state, opening up a phase of 'colonial state capitalism' that Low and Lonsdale have referred to as the 'second colonial occupation' (Low and Lonsdale 1976: III 12.) This ensured that post-colonial 'nation-building' would take on a pre-dominantly statist character. But the statist approach of the 'second colonial occupation' did not inaugurate developmental states as had earlier European or later East Asian capitalist development.

In fact, the 'second colonial occupation' was in part due to the intense competition from products coming from the United States, Japan and elsewhere that the British and the French faced in markets they dominated politically. In order to recoup the losses suffered in these transactions, the imperialists tried to pass on these losses to the African farmers, who had no way of resisting them. This led to a further monopolisation of the trading process in which colonial states were directly involved. During this period, European companies called on their governments to adopt an active policy to eliminate competition from small African traders who had emerged within the colonial economy. This is why a number of restrictive measures were imposed on African enterprise as the 'second colonial occupation' was being implemented. The period was also characterised by the importation into the colonies of large numbers of colonial technocrats, who devised development plans for each colony before they were granted political independence. The 'developmental state' was created to manage the colonial funding imported to 'modernize' the colonies in the post-war period.

This is also the context within which the allegedly positive achievements in the early post-colonial period must be assessed. It is argued by various writers that despite these postcolonial impediments to independent African development, achievements were quite impressive compared with other regions of the world. According to Mkandawire and Soludo (1999: 20), post-colonial African economic development attained 'fairly respectable rates of growth for nearly a decade'. Between 1965 and 1974, the annual growth in gross national product (GDP) averaged 2,6% across the continent. However, from 1974 onwards it stagnated, and by the end of the 1980s many African economies had a lower GDP per capita than at independence. According to Mkandawire and Soludo (1999: 20): 'This inverted-V pattern, with the apex over the mid-1970s, is true of virtually every economic indicator except agricultural output'. In the case of agriculture, the performance of this sector from 1955 to 1965 was quite high, but it too declined from the mid-1970s.

According to these two authors (ibid.: 21-40), the problem can be traced to the oil crises of 1973 and 1979. It was these developments that 'precipitated the recession in the developed countries, declining demand for raw materials, high interest rates, and so forth.' This is a simplistic approach. The oil crisis itself has to be explained within the context of the global economy at the time, which all the countries of the world faced. The question is why did this lead to recession in Africa, which was not overcome, while in other countries the situation was managed? Mkandawire and Soludo argue that the first sign of the 'impending crisis' was the increase in current account deficits 'as most African governments chose to finance continued expenditure through borrowing rather than adjustment' (ibid.: 21-22). But this can only be explained if you take into account the above analysis and the fact that world capitalism had to adjust to enable the multinational corporations that dominated African economies to squeeze even more from them.

In this regard, Manuel Castells correctly states that Africa's industrialization went into crisis: 'at exactly the same time when technological renewal and export-oriented industrialization' began to take root in other countries, especially South-East Asia. He adds that under these conditions, the survival of most African economies came to depend on international aid and foreign borrowing. But more significant was that this aid was not only from Western governments, but also from Western 'humanitarian donors', which increasingly became an 'essential feature of Africa's political economy' (Castells 2000: 87-88). In short, Castells says that while South-East Asian developmental states were able to move quickly to export-oriented industrialization, African post-colonial states were not. This can only be explained by their continued dependence on aid and humanitarian assistance for the survival of their people.

In these conditions, African 'developmental states' found themselves in a vicious circle. Unable to retain the resources generated by their economic activities, they became increasingly and permanently tied to external sources to finance whatever economic activity they planned. They could not create their own banking system to mobilise savings for export-oriented industrialization. This incapability is what led to the increased flow of aid to Africa, evidence of their dominated position in the global economy. The World Bank observed in this early period that the flow of external aid to Africa was larger, on a per capita basis, than that to Latin America or Asia. Africa had 22 per cent or $1,6 billion of the official bilateral and multilateral flows available to all Third World countries in 1967. This became necessary because of the huge resource outflows through monopoly over-pricing of its imports and under-pricing of its exports, which could not be retained internally. In the context of such weakness, it is necessary to be very precise in defining of what a 'develop-mental state' in Africa consisted in this period.

The restructuring of the African 'developmental state'

It can be seen that the situation in which most African economies found themselves in the period 1980-1990 was completely unsustainable. In 1979, African governments developed the Lagos Plan of Action calling for 'self-reliance', but this was doomed to failure since the states did not have the resources to implement it. This is what brought the World Bank to the attack. Beginning with the World Bank Berg Report of 1981, the African post-colonial state was re-theorised (World Bank, 1981) and the state blamed for all the ills that had befallen the earlier phase of economic and political development. The Berg Report came out following the World Bank 1979 Development Report, which had pointed to the engulfing crisis in Africa at the very time when African leaders were thinking of implementing a policy of self-reliance based on foreign support and assistance. The Berg Report blamed the 'slow growth of exports' for the crisis and pointed to many governmental 'policy biases'. This was necessary in order to push the new 'policy dialogue' that would enable the Bank to force African governments to restructure not only economies but also states.

But these new blueprints to get African countries to increase agricultural exports failed. Instead, the increases, if any, generated decreasing export incomes and increasing import prices. Faced with the failures of all the blueprints of the multilateral institutions, the World Bank in 1989 sought to provide a new and comprehensive theoretical and ideological position to push the process, alongside the failed political development, into an even more authoritarian mould under the guise of good governance. In its more professional and less polemical report, *From Crisis to Sustainable Growth*, the Bank developed what Beckman has correctly called 'a political theory of adjustment' (Beckman 1992: 83). The new report adopted a broader outlook by raising social, political and cultural issues in seeking to resolve the crisis. This was necessary in order to bring these states into line with the new globalising order. Unlike the earlier 'second colonial occupation', the 'third colonial occupation' took the form of privatisation and liberalisation of former state enterprises. State-run enterprises from the 'second colonial occupation' were dismantled.

This sell-off created new invasions of foreign capital, which took over former state enterprises at give-away prices. In the words of Beckman:

> The new focus of the World Bank is on the restructuring of the African state in order to make it supportive of its long-term strategy for the liberation of the market forces and entrepreneurial potentials of African society. The report explains the failure of the state and the need to cut it down to size, thereby releasing the creative forces that have suffered under its oppressive dead weight (Beckman 1992: 83).

The rationale of the new 'colonial occupation' was logical in its own terms. The African nation-state was a dead weight against the new economic and technological forces that were breaching national frontiers in terms of financial movements, trade flows and production strategies, as well as against its own people. Hence, the 'third colonial occupation' sought to put in place a neo-liberal ideology, which idealised the freedom of market forces vis-à-vis the previous economic role of the post-colonial state. By so doing it also tried to de-legitimise institutions of popular resistance against imperialism and neo-colonialism and to destroy the political achievements of the African people in their earlier resistance to colonialism. It was linked to a form of revisionist history that tried to restore the glory of colonial dependency under new conditions by highlighting the glory of the 'free market'!

Based on these analyses, the World Bank concluded that *the state must be made to retreat* in order to abide 'by the worldwide trend towards privatization' (IBRD 1989: 37-38, 4-5, 55). The logic was now inverted: instead of the state 'guiding' the market, under the 'third colonial occupation' the market had to 'guide' the state! Here the logic of the 'developmental state' was inverted. Thus the World Bank, in developing a political theory of adjustment, wanted to de-legitimise nationalism and nation-building and make the market the ultimate good under the guidance of the World Bank, the IMF and the donor community as far as Africa was concerned. This was also intended to attack civic organisations such as trade unions.

In the place of democracy, the World Bank developed the new concept of good governance, but this carried a different meaning to that of democracy. Private-sector initiative and market mechanisms must go hand-in-hand with good governance and so in the name of democracy a managerial concept of good governance and accountability became the new ideology of the market-state. But despite the new managerial state, by 2005 most African states, like some in South Asia and Latin America, were complaining of a huge debt overhang and calling for global debt cancellation and for Africa to have a fresh start with a line drawn under the past.

It can therefore be seen that under the Washington Consensus, as expressed in the 2005 World Development Report (World Bank 2004), the role of the state was merely to enhance the overall competitiveness of the private sector and let the business class determine the direction of investment. This it could do by increasing competitiveness principally through investment in infrastructure, education and training. In so doing, the state was instructed by the World Bank to avoid structural measures through 'targeted' policies that sought to promote particular sectors or types of ownership such as small enterprises. It was also enjoined not to control large sectors of the economy or direct credit to desirable activities. All this proved that the road to an Asian type of 'developmental state' and national economic transformation was closed in the era of globalisation.

Towards a glocal society in Africa

The glocal society arises from the reality of a globalising world informed by an informational and networked order. Information technology has linked countries spatially, with the result that the productivity and competitiveness of production units or agents in the economy fundamentally depend upon their capacity to generate, process and apply knowledge-based information efficiently. The globality of the economic system is based on the core activities of production, consumption and circulation being organised on a global scale, either directly or through a network of linkages between economic agents that are regionally, nationally and locally based. These conditions inform the emergence of the glocal system, with its components: the glocal state, the glocal market and the glocal society.

In characterising similar phenomena as 'glocalization,' Jordi Borja and Manuel Castells (1997: 214-216) point out that the emergence of the United Nations conferences and the experience of world and regional international organisations such as the World Bank, European Union, etc. 'have accorded new value to the local dimension in two main aspects: as the sphere of application of the integral policies (e.g. environment, economic promotion and social integration); and as a framework for concerted action by government bodies and private agents' (ibid.). They add that great value has, as a result, been attached to the principle of 'subsidiarity' or proximity of public administration, and to the participation or cooperation of civil society, a process that is today very closely linked with urbanisation: 'This is what has come to be known as glocalization, that is, links between the global and the local. ... This notion is today applied both to the economy ... and to culture (local identities and their dialectical relationship with media-based universalism of information, that is globalization plus proximity)'

(Borja and Castells 1997: 214).

The glocal state

There is no doubt that the character of the African post-colonial state, market and society-state relationship as crafted under European colonisation of Africa and its post-colonial reflection has proved, at great cost, unsuitable for Africa's development. In these circumstances to try to imagine or to reinvent and reform the post-colonial states in their present form is to try to imagine the impossible. What is required is a complete reorganisation of the state so that it has legitimacy among the people for whom it is supposed to promote development. Such a state has to respond to favourable global and local conditions that are part of our real world. It will not come about in a single 'bang' but through concerted struggles of ordinary people to form new states from below.

This means the existing post-colonial states should be dissolved after referenda are held in which people are consulted about the need to form new federated states. The decisions to dissolve the existing states then become irrevocable as the new federated states are constituted into one single federated state with inviolable regional borders, with the prospect of their expanding only by stages to include the rest of Africa. Such a transformation would be momentous because, for the first time, the people of Africa would have expressed *their sovereign will* to constitute states of their own in accordance with the modern reality of globality and locality. Some of the issues to be discussed leading up to the referendum should revolve around the new reality that would follow the dissolution of borders. These realities will include the fact that the new federal borders could not at any cost be undermined except through expansion to include other African communities. The call for a United States of Africa and the constitution of regional economic communities as 'building blocks' for such a United States cannot occur because it builds on structures that are decomposed or in the process of decomposition.

The glocal economy/market

The second need is for the state, however formed, to address the developmental needs of the entire population instead of sections of it. The globalisation of the world economy in conditions of delayed development has created a situation that is noticeably different from conditions in the developed economies. Since the imposition of structural adjustment programmes, the African post-colonial state has weakened further and the economic activities that we have referred to as 'informal' have actually become part of the globalised economy. They form part of the networks referred to above. Africa has become one of the fastest urbanising continents with the result that vast numbers of rural people are moving into megacities where the only economic activity is to join the 'reserve army' in the informal economy. These activities will eventually coalesce into new kinds of globally connected local economies.

The globalisation of economic forces has positively and negatively influenced the emergence of new flexible local economies and markets. In the 1989 report referred to above, the World Bank recognised that far from impeding future development strategy, 'many indigenous African values and institutions can support it'. It argued that while the 'modern sector' had been in depression in many African countries, the informal sector, 'strongly rooted in the community', had been 'vibrant.' In particular, according to the World Bank, this sector has shown a capacity 'to respond flexibly to changing circumstances' (IBRD 1989: 60). These changing circumstances include the growing relationship between the global economy and the generally survivalist informal sector based in local communities. However, for these linkages to be made more fruitful and positive for local actors, a reconstituted state must be supportive of local market opportunities instead of seeing them as 'illicit'. The Bank also argued that the modern sector 'should support the traditional sector, instead of seeking to replace it'. It therefore called for changes that are 'rooted in the country's social context', although it did not think of this as a strategic development. Currently, discussions are about how we can create sustainable economies and communities based on local resources and different forms of social capital, including indigenous knowledge. This is the way to go in the process of the emergence of a glocal economy.

The significance of the new glocal market is that it can build on existing social and intellectual capital in communities and develop new networks in the global economy. Apart from the resources of natural and indigenous knowledge referred to above, the African masses do have spiritual, cultural, physical and financial resources that they have accumulated throughout history and on which their communities are able to survive. Culture can no longer be looked at merely as dances and songs to entertain leaders at official ceremonies. Culture has always been a force for transformation and has formed the basis for African liberation and emancipation. It is now acknowledged to be an important political instrument for peoples' identity, self-definition and social transformation. The Peruvian economist Hernando De Soto has argued that identity is crucial to the market economy because it will not work if one has not got 'an infrastructure of identification'. He adds: 'If the population is split into two sections – Westernized and non-Westernized' – it is difficult for the market economy to be fully developed. Capitalism does not succeed only by having the correct 'macros in place, there is more to it than that and that is an identity system' (De Soto 2005). But we are now entering a new era, which can be described as post-capitalism, in which issues of identity and cultural integrity are at the core of demands for a new glocal order.

Some political economists have begun to see the importance of this connection between *social capital* and economic growth and development. There has been a revival of a debate in political and economic sociology, rooted in the work of Max Weber, Durkheim, Simmel and Marx, about the cohesion that social capital creates in small-sized countries. More recently, Woolock (1998) has criticised the way classical sociology used the concept of social capital and has elaborated the concept to analyse economic development in small-sized economies. Lundvall (2006) has argued that this analysis has implications for the present situation in many countries, its essential element being to dissolve the paradox of small countries that are caught up in the malaise of underdevelopment. He argues that such an approach recognises the role of 'social capital' in the broad sense used by Woolock above so that the state is supportive rather than undermining of the formation of social capital at local levels. Lundvall and Johnson (1994) also state the case for a 'learning economy' where the success of individuals, firms and regions depends on the capability to learn (and forget old practices), and in which there is a constant demand for new skills and for learning that includes the building of competences. This learning should go on in all parts of society, creating jobs in knowledge-intensive sectors.

Pan-African economic transformation is impossible without social transformation of the urban shanty economy as well as of the rural economy. For this a new model of economic and social transformation is necessary. There is also evidence, as the World Bank itself observed, of high savings taking place in 'informal' activities in Africa – in the order of 40% of domestic savings – in contrast to the high levels of 'capital flight' taking place in the 'formal' systems. This weakening in domestic investment and savings in formal systems is made worse by large-scale plunder and theft of public revenue, some of which is given as aid for African development.

In addition to informal sector savings, workers in Africa have large *pension funds*, which are invested in global financial markets, instead of in productive local activities. In South Africa alone, it is estimated that something close to 20 000 different workers' funds are available.

The total pension fund accumulation is estimated at R1,4 trillion. In most African countries the legislation concerning the use of these funds is undemocratic and there are continuous disputes between workers, employers and governments. In Uganda, the government received millions of dollars accumulated by the former East African Community workers, but instead of paying its nationals who had been employed there decided to put these funds to its own use. This goes on in other countries in different forms.

In contrast, the South-East Asian countries have used these funds for investment in local business ventures and community projects. In many parts of Africa, pension funds frequently find their way into Western money markets. Fund managers travel the continent in search of these funds and often bribe leaders for access to them. It is indefensible that a poor continent like Africa allows such large savings generated internally by the workers to leave the continent to benefit the rich world, while Africans are starving. There is a need to investigate these funds and work out a programme for their productive use in the countries where they are generated, while at the same time protecting the workers' interests and future needs. Civil society is well suited to carry out this study and organise advocacy work amongst the working class, businesses and governments to ensure the proper custody of the funds and their use for the transformation of the continent.

The glocal civil society

There is a discrepancy between the way 'civil society' is understood in Africa and the rest of the world.

In Africa the concept applies to a small group of urban-based, Westernised organisations. It does not include the majority of rural communities, which are still attached to their cultures and traditions. This is why the World Bank, while recognising the role of traditional society, nevertheless regarded it as not being part of civil society. It did this by emphasising the role of the 'intermediary classes' in adjustment programmes in Africa. The idea was to use these intermediary classes to co-opt groups engaged in informal activities so that they could be brought within the existing mainstream economic activities, which had failed to develop with the assistance of the state. In the World Bank's mistaken view, this was an 'empowering' intermediation. This is not sustainable because it under-estimates the capabilities of the 'rural' communities and their social and intellectual capital.

Hence, the new kind of glocal civil society must be inclusive of the urban and rural poor who have survived through informal activities. It must also include all members of society who struggle for the creation of a new glocal society. It should promote networks of people engaged in similar activities locally and globally. In this it would try to build a truly global citizenship based on inter-linked networks of local and global activity, in which the sum total of the local is what constitutes the global or the glocal. Indeed, this confirms the situation on the ground. An increasing number of the continent's population now live in peri-urban slums and these large numbers have been and are migrating from the countryside to the megacities to join the informal economy. What is needed is the recognition of this new glocal civil society that survives on local informal activities linked to the global economy, where society can develop a new development model in which its people are recognised as full citizens.

Conclusion

We have examined the role of the 'developmental state' in Africa and its ramifications for the people of Africa. We have seen that the expectation that the state would become developmental when the conditions for such a state did not exist negatively affected every facet of social and economic life on the continent. This included universities and other institutions of learning supposed to contribute to 'development' but which failed because of the malaise in the post-colonial states, leading to the present crisis in education. Embarking on investment in education without addressing the factors that have been responsible for Africa's 'underdevelopment' is therefore not the way to proceed.

This recognition leads us to see the importance of the 'learning economy' as a crucial aspect of a knowledge-based economy continuously emphasising *'learning to learn'* in different environments, since there is a strong connection between intellectual and social capital. This recognition implies that the future economy will be a function of two concurrent realities. At micro-level, the learning economy will be characterised by a change in the form of organisation towards functional flexibility. At macro-level, educational institutions will train students to *learn to learn* constantly and to form labour markets where there is balance between internal training and external mobility.

In relation to development strategies, this recognition points to the importance of social capital and to the need for investment in education and training that promotes the informal forms of the knowledge society. This is an important aspect of the new growth model, which can promote new forms of production and new markets. This will also propel development more fitted to self-reliance where social capital might increasingly become the scarce factor in the future. A new form of state and investment policy must work towards this new convergence, as Africa moves more and more into a learning economy based on its needs, but that also takes the needs of other communities into account in interlocking networks of economic and social relationships *glocally*.

References

Beckman, B. (1992) Empowerment or Repression? The World Bank and the Politics of African Adjustment. In Gibbon, P, Bangura, Y and Ofstad, A (1992). *Authoritarianism, Democracy and Adjustment: Politics of Economic Reform in Africa.* Seminar Proceedings No.26. Uppsala: The Institute of African Studies.

Borja, J and Castells, M. (1997) *Local and Global: Management of Cities in the Information Age.* London: Earthscan.

Castells, M. (2000) *End of Millennium.* Volume III, second edition. London: Butterworth. Davidson, B. (1992) *The Black Man's Burden: Africa and the Curse of the Nation-State.* London: James Curry.

De Soto, H. (2005) *The Mystery of Capital: Why Capitalism Triumphs in the West and Fails Everywhere Else.* New York: Basic Books.

Herring, RJ. (1999) Embedded particularism: India's failed developmental state. In Woo-Cumings, M (ed.). *The Developmental State.* Ithaca and London: Cornell University Press, 306-334.

IBRD. (1989) *Sub-Saharan Africa: From Crisis to Sustainable Growth.* Washington, DC: The World Bank.

Johnson, C. (1999) The developmental state: Odyssey of a concept. In Woo-Cumings, M (ed.). *The Developmental State.* Ithaca and London: Cornell University Press, 32-60.

Low, DA and Lonsdale, JM. (1976) Introduction: Towards the New Order 1945-1963. In Low, DA and Smith, A. (1976) *History of East Africa.* Volume III. Oxford: Clarendon Press.

Lundvall, B-A. (2006) Nation States, Social Capital and Economic Development: A System's Approach to Knowledge Creation and Learning. Development Research Series, Working Paper No.135, Institute for History, International and Social Studies, Aarlborg University, Norway.

Lundvall, B & Johnson, B. (1994) The learning economy. *Industry & Innovation,* 1(2): 23-42.

Mkandawire, T and Soludo, CG. (1999) *Our Continent: Our Future: Africa's Perspectives on Structural Adjustment.* Dakar: Codesria.

Sen, A. (1999) *Development as Freedom.* Oxford: Oxford University Press.

Vilakazi, H. (1999) The problem of African universities. In Makgoba, MW. (1999): *African Renaissance – The New Struggle.* Cape Town: Mafube Publishing Limited.

Woolock, M. (1998) Social capital and economic development: Toward a theoretical synthesis and policy framework. *Theory and Society,* 2(27): 151-207.

World Bank. (1981) *Accelerated Development in Sub-Saharan Africa.* Washington, DC: World Bank.

World Bank. (2004) *World Development Report 2005: A Better Investment Climate For Everyone.* Washington, DC: World Bank.

Contributors

Martin CARNOY is Professor of Education and Economics at Stanford University. He received his PhD from the University of Chicago, in the Department of Economics. Before moving to Stanford in 1969, he was a Research Associate at the Brookings Institution. He has written on issues of economic policy, theories of political economy, the economics of education, and educational policy. He has also written extensively on educational financing issues, including the effect of vouchers on educational outcomes. He consults regularly for the World Bank, the Inter-American Development Bank, and the Organisation for Economic Cooperation and Development on human resource policies.

Christopher COLCLOUGH is Professor of the Economics of Education and Director of the Centre for Commonwealth Education at Cambridge University. He was the founding Director of UNESCO's Global Monitoring Report on Education for All. Previously he was a Fellow (from 1975), and Professorial Fellow (from 1994) of the Institute of Development Studies at the University of Sussex. His research has concentrated on the economics of education in developing countries; education, planning and reform in Africa and Asia; gender and schooling in Africa; development theory and adjustment strategy. He has served as an adviser to UNICEF, UNESCO and the Rockefeller Foundation, and has served as a consultant to a wide range of agencies, including the World Bank, the UK's Department for International Development, the Norwegian Agency for Development Cooperation, and others, on general matters related to education and economic development.

Kenneth KING is Emeritus Professor of International and Comparative Education in the School of Education and the Centre of African Studies at the University of Edinburgh. His research and publishing interests have been in aid policy towards all sub-sectors of education; education and training in the informal sector; and on skills development, higher education, and knowledge policies. He has been Editor of *NORRAG News*, the aid policy review, for 20 years (www.norrag.org). He is a

Vice-President of the Royal African Society, and of the European Association of Development Research and Training Institutes. His current research, as part of the RECOUP Consortium, is on skills and poverty reduction. Since 2006, he has also been researching patterns of China-Africa cooperation, especially in education.

Keith LEWIN is the Director of the Centre for International Education and Professor in International Education and Development at the University of Sussex. He is a specialist in educational planning, the economics and financing of education, teacher education, and science and technology education policy in developing countries. He has extensive experience in south and south-east Asia, China, and southern Africa. He is a consultant on educational planning and finance to governments in Africa and Asia, and to a range of development agencies including the World Bank, UNICEF, UNDP, UNESCO, the Asian Development Bank, the UK's Department for International Development (DFID), and the Deutsche Gesellschaft für Technische Zusammenarbeit (German Technical Cooperation), or GTZ. He is the Director of the DFID supported Consortium for Research on Educational Access, Transitions and Equity (CREATE), and was President of the British Association for International and Comparative Education in 2005-06.

Dani NABUDERE is the Executive Director, Principal and Honorary Senior Research Fellow of the Marcus Garvey Pan Afrikan Institute at Mbale, Uganda. Professor Nabudere was the Director of the Yiga Ng'Okola Folk Institute, an NGO for Women's Empowerment, from 1993 to 2000. He is a former Minister of Justice in the Ugandan Government, and also Minister of Culture, Community Development and Rehabilitation. He is a Past President of the African Association of Political Science, and Vice-President of the International Political Science Association. He has written several books, chapters and articles on imperialism and international finance. His recent research has included work on the war in northern Uganda, the Lords' Resistance Army, historical memory and reconciliation in Uganda, and traditional techniques of conflict resolution and management.